Breaking Up
is Hard to Do

by Patrick Bond
Series editor: Joan King

Written by Patrick Bond

Series editor: Joan King

Cover design by Phillip Vernon

Published by:
National Christian Education Council
1020 Bristol Road
Selly Oak
Birmingham
B29 6LB

British Cataloguing-in-Publication Data:
A catalogue record for this book is available from the British Library.

ISBN 0-7197-0981-4

First published 2000

©2000 Patrick Bond

Patrick Bond has asserted his right under the Copyright, Designs and Patents Act, 1988, to be identified as Author of this Work.

All rights reserved. No part of this publication may be reproduced, stored in a retrieval system, or transmitted in any form or by any means electronic, mechanical, recorded or otherwise, without the prior permission of the publisher.

Typeset by the National Christian Education Council
Printed by Biddles, Guildford, UK

Contents

Acknowledgements................................ 5
Preface.. 6
Introduction..................................... 7

How to Believe in Anything?...................... 12
Before the Break-up............................. 24
Beginning the Break-up.......................... 27
The Egg of Darkness............................. 30
The False Dawn.................................. 33
The Estranged World............................. 36
Looking Back to Look Forwards................... 39
The Wilderness Choice........................... 43
The Volcano of Anger............................ 54
Love and Pain................................... 62
Men and Divorce................................. 66
Children: Responsibility and Agony.............. 75
Healing, Restoration and the Discipline of Love. 86
Conclusion...................................... 94
Further Reading................................. 96

Acknowledgements

I would like to thank the Management Committee of the Dawn Project, my employers, and Rachel Ross, my line manager, for supporting me through the process of writing this book. Technical contributions came from Revd Kevin Barnard of the Sheffield Diocese, for the theological reflections, and from Jo Saville of Rotherham Women's Refuge, for the information on domestic violence. However, I have adapted the contributions in my own way; hence, all opinions expressed in the book are entirely my own responsibility.

I am eternally grateful to those people, colleagues, friends and acquaintances, who filled in my questionnaire. They had the courage to face and explore the pain of their own break-ups, and then write it all down for me. They shall remain anonymous, but I owe them a debt of gratitude.

I am conscious of debts to my teachers, over the years. To Peter Weir, dedicated, principled and inspiring teacher in my school days; to the late Stephen Booth Harris, a generous friend—and someone who believed in me, during a painful period of my life; to Keith Tudor and Louise Embleton Tudor, of Temenos in Sheffield, for the rigorous immersion in the philosophy of Carl Rogers, whose influence may be felt throughout this book. And also to the great teachers I have met only through their books, Carl Jung and Paul Tillich.

Finally, I owe thanks to my wife, Liz, for encouraging me, supporting me through weeks of effort, and remaining engaged in the subject matter of the book with me. It was in many ways a shared endeavour. My children and step-children have also taken the strain, and I am grateful to Jonathan, Aidan, Thomas, Ellie, Sophie and Amy for their love, patience and goodwill.

Preface

This book is one in a series called *Family Change* published by the National Christian Education Council as part of its *Faith in the Future* initiative. Each book in the series focuses on a major transition that many adults face and helps us to face the realities of the experience and to learn from them. In this book we take a subject that is increasingly part of people's experience—the process of separation and divorce.

Marriage is popular. So is the process of uncoupling, or separating, or so it may seem. The media headlines 'scream' statistics at us. One in three marriages will end in divorce. The average length of a marriage is 9.8 years. Women initiate seventy per cent of all divorces. And these statistics, which vary slightly by the day, do not incorporate those of cohabiting couples who may be engaged in a process of separating too!

As Neil Sedaka and Howard Greenfield made powerfully clear in their famous song *Breaking Up is Hard to Do*, it is a complex and difficult process that no one finds easy. Behind the statistics are people—women, men and children as well as their networks of family and friends. All are affected by a break-up.

Statistics are blunt tools that are of use to social scientists, planners and politicians but they say little about the social, community reality of marriage or committed partnership, still less about the inner, emotional reality of those doing the breaking up. In this book Patrick Bond tackles this—the inner reality of breaking up or how it feels from 'within'. Through it he helps those involved to understand themselves better, to recognize that different people have found themselves in similar emotional places during the process of uncoupling and, perhaps most importantly, he offers hope to those involved. Through the pain and hard times there is the hope of change and growth, and of finding oneself in a better place even though some of the scars of the experience may remain.

I am sure that the book is of relevance to those who are going through, or have been through, the process of separation and divorce. As someone who has not done so, I have found my insight enhanced in ways that may help me to be more understanding and supportive of friends and family who have done so. And so I recommend the book to others like me.

Joan King
Series Editor

Introduction

In some strange way, I knew about the break-up some four years before it happened, but something in me shut it out of sight. It was something too terrible to look at. It could not happen to me!

I was first married when I was just twenty. My wife was eighteen. We had 'gone out' for three years, and that seemed a long time to wait!

Within five years there were two children, and problems. But we were young, and optimistic. Within ten years, another child, and the marriage had started to collapse, but I could not see it. At twelve years the problem was out in the open, and I had no way to deal with it. Two years later we separated.

My attitude to marriage was firmly based in all the religious teachings I had absorbed, about the sacredness of marriage, the indissoluble bond, the vows that could never be revoked. From society I received the message that marriage was part of the glue that held everything together. From my community, I received the message that everything was worthwhile, 'for the sake of the children'. When it came to the crunch, none of that helped much.

In a sense, my powerful urge to 'make it work' was my undoing. My determination to absorb pain, and make the best of it, made me blind to what I was really doing, and to what my wife was doing. I held on to an interpretation of reality, and real life passed me by. I did not see what was coming.

For nine years after the separation, I could not bring myself to put through a divorce. The marriage 'ideal' was so firmly rooted in me that I could not bear to break the cord, even long after the marriage partnership had ended and the relationship had become totally changed.

Three years after my divorce, and following a lot of personal development work, I see marriage quite differently. I am married again, and I now know that my first marriage, while it was intense and committed, was not a real relationship. I have found a real relationship, and there is no comparison between the two. I am intensely sorry that I assisted in perpetuating something so unreal, for so many years. That pain will always be with me. However, I do not regret anything. There was joy and incredible togetherness, as well as anger and betrayal, on both sides. We were two young people who did the best we could. Our children were, and are, beautiful.

Introduction

I am writing this book to pay tribute to that marriage, and to all marriages where people try hard and honestly to do the best they can. But I am writing primarily for those who come to the moment of breaking up, to convey my belief that there is something positive in this experience, beyond the collapse of ideals and hopes, beyond mere survival, and beyond bitterness and recrimination.

The Book

This book explores, in an organic and non-theoretical way, my experience and that of many others. It is not a 'how to' book about divorce—see the booklist for help with that. There is no 'magic wand' that can be waved over the pain and sadness, and no theoretical perspective that can suddenly make everything clear. There is only the mystery of why we have to face such a degree of pain, how we get through it, and how we come to understand the meaning of what has happened. There is also the mystery of our own inner growth through this painful experience, the complexity which replaces our more simple outlook when younger, and the multi-coloured pattern of a more mature way of loving, which replaces the bright primary colours of first love.

The focus of the book is on the pain of separation and divorce. This may not seem a very cheerful approach! However, I believe that pain is a gateway for each of us, rather than a rock on which we are wrecked. Also, I assume that this book has come to you because you want more than a superficial pat on the shoulder. I assume that you want some way of seeing the truth of what has happened to you, and a method of finding your own way through something that may seem incomprehensible. I hope you will find my approach helpful.

I believe that we experience life in its emotional realities, and in moments of awareness, rather than in theories about living. I am interested in the moments of choice. Often we are totally free to choose one way or another: free to choose paths that lead to facing pain or hiding from it, taking on the consequences or dumping them onto others, expanding our outlook or shrinking it down, moving on to new experience or repeating old cycles. There is a deep mystery in those moments of choosing, and the choices we make govern our life direction at a profound level.

My attitude to the making of choices is that people do the best they can, in their own life circumstances. Preaching at them does little good, and may make them hostile. My belief is that fundamental principles of loving respect for oneself and others, honest communication, and a sensitive reaching out in relationships, are the keys to a journey of self-discovery and faith. In case my language seems unduly distant from the standard Christian approach, I have to say that I long ago found that the words

Introduction

used by Christian teachers and thinkers had become (in the main) meaningless to me—not because they lack truth, but because they have become a technical jargon which tends to exclude more people than it includes. I found I needed to translate them, to get at the truth which would otherwise remain hidden.

So I use a language and a model in which relationship is primary; where change and inner growth are vital to spiritual life; where feelings and intuitions are trustworthy; where mutuality, not imposed authority, is the touchstone, and where there is no such thing as failure, only experience. My relationship with myself, with my partner, and with God, is characterized by development and change, by open communication, respect and sharing, and by a mutual valuing, trust and acceptance. It is a philosophy that emphasizes the present not the future, and lets me be unafraid of pain, open to joy, and alive to love. It is not easy.

The Reader

Whether you were formally married, or have been in a committed, long-term partnership, there seems to me to be little difference in the personal, emotional impact of separation or divorce. The pain is the same, and the challenges equally severe. I am not saying that formal marriage is meaningless. I believe that marriage does make an essential difference to a relationship. It is a solemn, formal declaration and affirmation of the relationship, and if the marriage service is religious, there is a sacramental dimension for the committed Christian believer.

But emotionally, the impact of breaking up is the same, and I propose to treat the breaking-up process in the same way, whether it applies to a formal marriage or a partnership, and whether the basis is religious or secular. There are theological reflections on marriage and divorce towards the end of the book. While I refer to 'men and women' throughout the book, I believe that the emotional realities of breaking up may be the same for any sexual orientation. If this is an oversimplification, then I apologize to any group that finds itself misrepresented. The position I take is also influenced by my white background, and the problems I discuss may therefore have less relevance to people with a different cultural inheritance.

The Process of Breaking up

The emphasis throughout the book is on breaking up as a process, not as an isolated, tragic event. The advantage of this is that we can see it as a series of choices and possibilities, not as a series of endings and discontinuities. Yes, there are endings, and the tragedy of failed hopes and dreams; but there are also

Introduction

choices which can lead to new beginnings. While every partnership, and every break-up, is unique to the people involved, there are still processes of relationship breakdown which are common to many marriages, and processes of healing which many people can vouch for in the aftermath.

I tend to look at relationships, rather than love. 'Love' is a word so personal in its meanings that it can mean many things to many people. I believe that loving resides in the heart, not in the relationship. When a relationship dies, the possibility of loving remains with you. No one can take love from you, though they may cease to love you in the same way. Love seems to me to be based in the openness of the human spirit to new experience and new life.

My focus is on the central freedom you possess in life—your freedom to choose in the moment, and to grow—and what you can do to increase the positive potential of every choice you make. I define 'positive' as something that is more accurately suited to your unique personality and identity, as opposed to something you feel you 'ought' to do, or must believe in.

I assume that, whether you left or were left, your intentions were basically caring, not malicious: in other words, that you were seeking to cause as little damage as possible, and that hurt and pain were essentially secondary to your main intention, and unavoidable. I see anger as legitimate, in relieving the pressure of your feelings; but I do not accept that malice and an intention to harm have any part to play in a relationship, whether on-going or in the past.

I see 'breaking up' both as a process and as part of a process. I look at the process of breaking up—its stages, as far as it can have recognizable stages. I also look at breaking up as itself a part of your life process, which can lead you to new experience, growth, and deeper wisdom.

I also give alternatives to the negative impulses we all experience. There are responses to the pain and damage which are more positive, and some which are less positive: you will be able to see alternatives, and this may help to reduce the confusion and panic. There are suggestions for protecting you, nurturing your gentle side, strengthening your ability to look after yourself and your loved ones, and turning to face a new future, instead of a past which has ended.

Introduction

Pain and Freedom

One obvious omission from the book is any direct mention of forgiveness. In my own life experience, I have had to wrestle with the idea of forgiveness, and I have come to the conclusion that I cannot 'forgive', if that means I have to make judgements about who is to blame. I feel that I do not have the right to say that someone else has 'done me harm', which I then have to forgive. All I can truthfully say is that I felt pain in certain situations, and that I was part of what happened. In this way of looking at it, blaming someone else and trying to 'forgive' them is not useful if it seems to put me 'above' them.

Instead, I can choose to work at recognizing some of the harm that I have done in the past (mostly without knowing it at the time) and apologize. I can also respond positively if someone asks me for forgiveness, but I am not in a position to say that I know precisely what the 'harm' was, or who was to blame. I do not think of myself as someone who can decide who did what, and to whom, and how, and how much. The whole question of good and evil, blame and punishment, is beyond my limited powers.

What I can do, however, is respect other people's freedom to be themselves, and respect my own freedom to be myself. The real ethical challenge is in balancing these two forms of profound respect, in deepening my awareness of what is really going on when I relate to someone, and in renewing my sense of trust in the discoveries which life brings before me.

Pain—Gateway to the Future

In the moment of accepting pain, there comes also the moment of moving beyond terror, into a new, complicated life full of new horizons and different joy—and, probably, different pain! But the pain will always be my signal, or gateway, that I can look further than the usual horizon, and move forward into somewhere new. Forgiveness, to me, is a state of honest respect for another person, and for oneself too. In this sense, the whole book is about how to find a way beyond pain and blame, to positive forgiveness and joyful acceptance.

How to Believe in Anything?

Marriage breakdown and divorce may be common nowadays, but nothing prepares you for the shock of when it happens to you. Nothing in society, or community, or church prepares you. No amount of stories you have heard from friends, or dramas you have watched on TV or films, makes any difference. You can hide behind any number of masks or roles or jobs, but the inner challenge is always the same. Do you really believe you can make it on your own? Do you really believe in YOU? Where do you find your strength? Everything in you screams that it is not fair, that this should not happen to you, that you have failed—'You are a failure'. You have failed to make the grade. All the sour predictions of parents and teachers seem to have come true. 'You'll live to regret that'; 'You'll learn the hard way'. It all seems like a nightmare that has come true. The pain is intense, and indescribable.

Or maybe you saw it coming, but always hoped you could fend it off, fight against the flow, hold on until the problems were cured...? You may have hung on to a grim sense of heroism, just gritting your teeth and battling on, in the best British stiff-upper-lip tradition.

Perhaps it seemed 'strong' to put up with lack of real communication with your partner, unpleasantness, rows and even betrayal, and hope for better times in the future. It may be that you stayed together 'for the sake of the children' or you simply refused to believe that you would become just another statistic in the figures for marriage breakdown!

What do you hold on to? There are choices to be made now, and urgently, but all your choices that led to this have been proved faulty. How do you make the hard choices now? How do you believe in anything, and above all, how do you believe in yourself?

These are the heart-rending questions that come when divorce or partnership breakdown becomes a reality. Few people understand what is involved. Few people want to know about the pain, the shock, the inner turmoil, the anger, or the fear. This book is written for all those who have been touched by the pain of separation and divorce, and want to know that there is a future beyond the agony and the grief.

I begin with the stories of nine women shared through their replies to a questionnaire devised by me. They are followed by other stories at various places throughout the book, including those of five men in the chapter 'Men and Divorce'. The stories will help us to touch the realities of the respondents' feelings during their processes of breaking up with their partners. I am profoundly grateful to all those people who helped in this way, for their courage in putting painful memories into writing, and for their trust in me. All specific details and names have been changed, to preserve anonymity.

Nine Women's Stories

How did you learn about the break-up? How long ago? Did you initiate it?

1. I knew a long time before the break-up that it was going to happen—from the time I realized it wasn't going to work, I think I behaved in ways that led up to it. It happened eight years ago. I initiated the break-up.

2. After being terribly concerned as to my husband's health, and questioning him, he told me he had been having an affair for three and a half years, pre-dating the birth of our second child. It happened nearly ten years ago. I did not initiate the break-up.

3. I first knew something was going to happen when I found myself collecting together important documents, such as my passport, MOT certificate, birth certificate. I asked myself what on earth I was preparing myself for. It happened five years ago. I initiated the break-up.

4. My ex-husband told me the day he left. It happened four years ago. I did not initiate the break-up.

5. I learned about it from my ex-husband. It happened twelve years ago. I did not initiate the break-up.

6. I learned about it by living with it (the violence). I initiated the break-up.

7. By gradual realization: a growing suspicion that the relationship was near its end. It happened seven years ago. I initiated it, once I had the courage to admit to myself that it was over.

8. My husband told our priest that he was having an affair and asked him to break the news to me. He stayed in the marital home for the next two years and four months. In the meantime, he finished his affair and started another one. He rang me one afternoon, and said that he had seen some accommodation and he was going to move out of the marital home at the end of the week. It happened

fourteen years ago. I did not initiate the break-up, but I do remember saying that it was about time he chose what he was going to do—leave, or decide to make a go of it with me.

9. My second marriage ended ten years ago. I had started a second family and had a young child aged two. The break-up was partly due to the fact that my husband did not want to change his lifestyle even though we had a young child. I also believe there were mental health problems that may have caused a breakdown. When I asked our GP for clarification on this, he said he was unable to give me any information about my partner due to confidentiality.

What made you most angry?

1. What made me most angry was the feeling that it could have been different if he'd been willing to change. I don't feel angry in that way now.

2. Deceit, manipulation, and degradation suffered through the marriage.

3. At the time just before leaving my husband, I was most angry with God. I adored my husband, and found myself falling in love with another man with whom I wanted to live. I begged God not to let it happen, to intervene in his love for me.

4.

5. I felt little anger.

6. Violence, him blaming me, his lies, meanness, selfishness. The suffering of the children.

7. My partner's opinion that he had a 'right' to continue our relationship.

8. I can't say I was angry about the break-up. It was afterwards that anger kicked in, when he tried to duck out of his responsibilities—financial and moral.

9. The hurt came from the feelings of being betrayed, let down, humiliated and a feeling of guilt that I had failed to make a second marriage work.

What made you most hurt?

1. I felt most hurt around issues to do with the children. I felt he had not been a good father to them.

2. That he did not love me: my efforts had been in vain.

3. My leaving my husband devastated and angered many, many people, and this hurt me, because I knew how confused they all were. A colleague, with whom I had worked for many years, wrote to inform me that I had now lost God, my husband and my children. That hurt profoundly!

4. The fact that I was ill in hospital and my husband was carrying on with my so-called best friend.

5. That he didn't love me any more, and that my son was losing his father.

6. That he treated me, and spoke to me, like something he trod in. That I allowed him to.

7. The fact that I was not being listened to or cared about by him.

8. The fact that he had betrayed our relationship to an outsider. It may sound strange but I think I would have preferred it if he had had an affair with someone I knew.

9.

What made you most fearful?

1. I was afraid of being on my own for the rest of my life. I felt most fearful of not being able to make a real relationship ever.

2. Dealing with a person I didn't know, i.e. my husband. Losing control. Money. Dying without resolving everything, and securing the children.

3. I had been married to my husband for 25 years, he was my one love, and the fear of being without him felt at times as if it would overpower me. Death continued to feel preferable.

4. Being on my own with the kids and being poorly for six to eight months after the break-up with no help at all.

5. The future, living on my own, and the thought I would never meet anyone else who would love me.

6. Knowing what he was capable of, for my children. Making me feel vulnerable and worthless.

How to Believe in Anything?

7. His threats of suicide.

8. How I would manage to bring up the children on very little money.

9. As with my first marriage breakdown, some of my fears were around decisions about where I would live, arrangements for child-minding to enable me to continue working, and major decisions around property and possessions.

Did you ever feel very low? If so, when?

1. I felt very low sometimes while I was on my own with the children—wondering how I would cope with a full-time job and two young children's needs and my own.

2. After a year or so. After the adrenaline anger had burnt out, and I felt I was going nowhere, treading water.

3. It is hard for me to say what hurt the most, I was in so much pain, I was barely functioning and couldn't eat. I tried to talk to my husband, but it was useless. At the time just before leaving him … I was so low, I desperately wanted to be dead, the only thing that kept me going was my daughter's grief should I leave her completely.

4. Yes, all the time.

5. All of the time, every day I was on my own I felt very sad (about two years).

6. Many, many times during most of the thirty years of marriage. Depressed. Suicidal many times.

7. When I believed we might actually stay together to stop him committing suicide.

8. Two years after he left, without warning me, he changed from paying the maintenance into my account on a monthly basis to weekly payment by cheque. It threw my budget into chaos and I felt like putting the children in the car and driving it into a wall. I was at the stage that, as long as I had regular maintenance, I could cope with everything else.

9. The death of my ex-husband (some time after we divorced) brought about other feelings of grief and loss which affected me quite deeply but have enabled me to help other people talk through some of the issues of grief and loss through either death or divorce.

What kept you going?
1. What kept me going was my faith and belief in my relationship with the children. Despite everything, I felt I was providing the essential nurturing they needed and that the decision to separate had been as much for their benefit as mine, i.e. we were in a better place than before.

2. Dogged determination, anger, a good friend, my brother, lovely children.

3. Nothing was helpful, except the love of my new partner.

4. The kids.

5. My son, mostly, and when I met my present husband I could hope again for the future.

6. Three children, prayers, God.

7. Determination, which also felt like optimism and a belief in the future.

8. Friends, church, family, but most of all, the children. I had to keep going for their sakes.

9.

What was your best source of help?
1. My relationship with my children gave me support. They trusted me to a huge degree. Some friends were supportive too.

2. Inwardly: self worth. Outwardly: family backing.

3. Most helpful was that he (my partner to be) never made any promises to me. He did not try to rescue me in the sense of finding me somewhere to live. I did that for myself. I got a job to keep myself, and received no financial help from my husband.

4. There was none.

5. Good friends and family because they knew both of us, and understood the depth of hurt we were feeling.

6. Children, church, Relate, AA, local Domestic Violence Unit, friends.

7. Friends and therapy.

8. Friends, church, family, my children—and prayer.

9.

What do you regret most?
1. I regret not having had the self-awareness, experience and depth to work at the relationship without fear.

2. Living through a damaging relationship—but I don't regret my children!

3. I regret that I did not understand what was happening to me at the time, and why I was falling in love. My need for a close intimate relationship based on honesty and someone's desire not only to be with me, but to know me, was the cause of my leaving. I regret that I only knew a very little of myself when I was with my ex-husband; had I known more, maybe I could have been honest years ago, and we might have created a relationship which would have been more like the one I now have.

4. Marrying the bastard, and leaving my home-town.

5. That I missed two years of my son's growing up because I was so unhappy in my situation.

6. Not leaving sooner when the children were younger.

7. My ex-partner is the father of our son. Obviously, I don't regret that, but I do regret that I haven't given my son a stable family and two loving parents.

8. That the children haven't had a loving father to share their lives.

9. My main regrets are that we were unable to talk and discuss our problems in order to resolve some of the conflict and resentment between us. We did go some way to repair some of the relationship eventually, when he became ill with cancer, from which he later died.

Are you in a better place now?
1. Yes. I have learned a lot and developed a real relationship in which I feel I and the children thrive.

2. Yes. I knew it was possible and I treasure the peace it brings.

3. The place I am in now means I have discovered more about myself. It is better, but the grief I have for what my ex-husband and I missed, is still in my heart, like a very cold, dark nail in a coffin, the lid of which is closed tightly. Inside are treasured memories, beautiful dreams, the birth of our children, the love we shared, the laughter, my fear, his fear, an awful lot of stress, and a river of tears. And at the moment, I think God is in there too!

4. Yes.

5. Yes!

6. Cannot say. Too many emotions, still quite raw.

7. Yes, infinitely.

8. Yes, yes, yes.

9. Yes. I am now in a third marriage, and my partner is a wonderful father to my daughter and a loving husband to me.

What did the experience give you?

1. The experience gave me learning for life—wisdom—determination to know myself better, to understand the meaning of my life. I had a taste of the pain in life.

2. Compassion. It humbled me. I felt degraded at first but latterly a feeling of pride, status, power: I had survived and the kids were OK. A different perspective on relationships. A critical look at where I had come from. Qualification to understand other people's situations in my work, teaching, and so on. It taught me how to set goals for myself to recover or re-invent myself. It felt likehurdling, or planning a campaign. It taught me that distress causes physical frailty, e.g. rapid weight loss initially. It gave me benchmarks for new relationships. It gave me new friends and I also lost friends. (The experience can polarize friendships: somepeople fear you and others become intimate).

3. The experience has given me a compassion for those who are in spiritual and marital crisis. Most of all, it has given me my present partner, who wants to know me, who has the courage to stay with me, and wants me to know and stay with him, the pain, the joy and the fear.

How to Believe in Anything?

4. Strength to cope with most of what life can throw at me.

5. Inner strength that I didn't know I had, and a greater understanding of men and their needs in a relationship. I think I was too complacent in my first marriage. I didn't see that my husband was unhappy until it was too late. This has made me work harder at this marriage, and develop myself more as an individual rather than somebody's wife.

6. Cannot say yet. My head is not together right. Hope it soon will be.

7. Headaches, a big overdraft, unhappiness and guilt! (Plus the ability to be myself, and a greater idea of who that might be.)

8. Self-knowledge, deeper friendships, humility, self-respect, and an understanding of why people steal, or abuse themselves through drink or prostitution.

9. I do feel that I have now come out of the other side of the tunnel and have developed as a person through my experiences. I feel I am more tolerant and that I am able to listen to others' points of view. It has helped me to have an understanding of lots of different difficulties facing families, and this has helped me in my work situation. Through my experiences, I am trying to give my daughter opportunities for self-development that will give her an inner strength and an understanding of other people's choices and problems, and to give her a caring attitude to life.

One Woman's Story

I am including this story on its own, because many issues are touched upon, and conveyed more directly than any summarizing or theorizing of mine could achieve!

How did you learn about the break-up? How long ago? Did you initiate it?

This feels complicated to answer. Intuitively, I knew after my partner of twelve years, and husband for six, returned from a business trip abroad. He had left a message on our answerphone to say that he would telephone before the children's bedtime, and then was missing for thirty-six hours afterwards. He did not telephone, and had his mobile switched off. We went to Relate in June. I cried throughout the session and said that I believed that he wanted to leave but that he needed to say this in front of a witness. He was amused by this.

In fact, for every day of the next three months he told me that he was leaving the next day, the next week, and so on. It became like torture.

In the end, after a summer of calling me back home whenever I was away, on the pretext that he was leaving, I asked him to leave. It happened that, on my way home from a training course, I telephoned home in case I would miss speaking to the children before they went to bed. There was pandemonium. I spoke to my son who said that his father had head-butted him across the nose before school that morning. He had gone to school with a nose-bleed and a suspected broken nose, and as he was speaking to me, I could hear his father in the same room laughing. I returned home and insisted that he should now leave, as he had been insisting was his intention. I felt that if I did not insist, I would be unable to leave the children with him when I attended my training course the following fortnight later. I feared that they could end up on an 'at risk' register.

I guess the short answer is that I intuitively knew. I guess that I first knew that it was happening a couple of days after we met! But at the end I was told that he was leaving, on a daily basis, for three months or so. The night that he left I knew for the first time that I had no other course of action but to set in place irretrievably a physical ending of eighteen years.

What made you most angry?

About the specific break-up? Cowardice. The man said that he wanted to go, and I can understand how difficult it is to leave. I can understand how very difficult it was for him to leave. He just could not do it on his own. He did not know whether to go or to stay. He did not know how to make his mind up. In the end he knew somewhere inside him that if he hurt one of the children, it would be all over, and that's what he did. He has referred to it since as his one mistake, but I think that there was a lot going on behind it.

What made you most hurt?

I was most hurt that he seemed to have no will to save anything, to find out if things could work. I realize now that that was not new, it was my understanding and accepting of it that was new. I was hurt that it was his 'experiencing of not being loved now' which had made him realize just how much he had been loved once. (These are his words.) I was hurt that he did not connect his 'feeling unloved' with me, enough to say, 'I wonder if this is what she must be feeling like, never receiving this from me', and attempt to remedy it. He had always said that he was incapable of offering love, did not know what it was. I was also hurt by two one-liners: 'You were a one-night stand that went on for eighteen years' and 'Now that I have resolved issues around my mother's death, I am ready for a divorce'. She died when he was seven years old, and it sounds as if I had never existed to him as myself, but only as his mother.

What made you most fearful?
I was most fearful that the children would become extremely distressed, individually and collectively, and that I would need to be strong enough to support them in their grief, in an appropriate way for each.

I was also fearful that the children and I would have to find somewhere else to live, and that financially things would collapse.

I was also physically fearful of him. After a second trip away, I realized that I was becoming increasingly anxious about when he would return and how he would be. On one day my energy completely drained, and I began to shake violently and become very tearful. I had begun to see him as totally unpredictable and not known to me. I had a sense that violence could be brewing, but I never anticipated that he would hurt one of the children. He had a history of injuring himself deliberately, some years ago.

Did you ever feel very low? If so, when?
I felt very low throughout last summer. It felt like torture. Lots of uncertainty. Lots of unknown. And pure grief that all hope was at an end.

What kept you going?
The children who were so delightfully 'normal' throughout. Friends who said things like, 'You're strong'. And the neighbour who volunteered, 'You've always kept that family together, you're the strong one'.

A gay neighbour who I guess I thought would have sympathies with the man in the relationship, who made me laugh by saying, 'Get rid of him, you're worth more. Get his key back and say, "From now on, you stop at the wall"', and who still waves to me every day as he passes, checking that I'm still OK.

Other people locally, whose partners had left unexpectedly, were very supportive. Friends who came around after the children had gone to bed and cuddled me and rocked me. Meditation. It was in David Brazier's first Buddhist book, *Zen Therapy*, that I read, 'Life is full of pain, pain is inevitable, but suffering is optional'. Do I want to hold on to the pain and suffer, or do I want to experience the pain, accept it and its lessons for me, and then move on?

What was your best source of help?
Mindfulness. I broke down one day with my friend, and this tender, lovely man simply said to me, 'Take care of yourself. Be mindful' and I knew what he meant. Live in this moment. Do not allow the fear, and all the 'what ifs' of future moments to cloud how I am in these. I may never live to experience the 'what ifs'. I do, however, want to experience, engage with, delight in, enjoy, my 'nows'. My friends, who always offered encouragement, cuddles, money, lifts to the supermarket, and another pair of hands at the other end of putting up heavy shelves.

My counsellor, who shared of herself in very empathic and supportive ways.

Meditation has been a help, especially the Metta Bhava.

What do you regret most?
I regret deeply that our son was hurt. But I believe that the hurt for him started a long time ago, otherwise this would not have happened between them. I regret that too.

I regret not becoming more aware earlier, although my counsellor chides me gently for this. I felt honourable in the break-up, no matter what went before.

Are you in a better place now?
Much better, thank you. I feel more content within myself than ever before. I feel energized. (I did not know just how much energy is drained from one, living with someone who has long-term depression.) Although looking tired, I feel vibrant much of the time.

What did the experience give you?
First-hand experience of gut-wrenching, heart-thumping, fear-inspiring grief. It also showed me that each of my children was and is a lot more capable than I had thought. A more focused lesson in mindfulness! The knowledge that no matter what comes my way, if I truly engage with it, experience it, accept it, it will pass and I shall move forward. I did not die from it! That I am capable on my own, if restricted—I am resourceful and practical. I feel funny about saying this, since I do like me! It also gave me the knowledge that despite words back and forth over the years, this man and I were just not right for one another, and neither of us can help that. I thought that we had been soul mates, ports in a storm, but that was my delusion.

Before the Break-up

What happens in the long process that leads to break-up? I am thinking of times when we may be unaware of any particular failure in the relationship: just a nagging feeling that things are not right. There are certain ideas and attitudes which we tend to call upon, in the attempt to understand or rationalize what we are feeling, and hold things together. These are what I offer below, in the form of commonly-used phrases, along with a fresh look at what we really mean by them. Like most wise sayings, they contain more than a grain of truth, but there is always room for us to be more precise and self-aware. Not all marriages lead to divorce where people use such explanations and descriptions but, where breaking up turns out to be inevitable, this 'spiral' is a reasonable sketch of one common process. I call it a spiral, because it seems (with hindsight) to lead to one end, while appearing at the time always to lead somewhere else. How often have you heard these phrases, or ones like them?

- 'We're OK really.'
- 'We are a bit rocky sometimes.'
- 'I'm used to it now.'
- 'We have our ups and downs: doesn't everybody?'
- 'We had a bad patch, but we've made up now.'
- 'We are both really trying.'
- 'Something has changed between us: maybe it's just time passing.'
- 'You just have to plod on, sometimes.'
- 'It could be worse.'
- 'The children have got to come first.'
- 'I'm not one to run away from a challenge.'
- 'I'm not a loser: I'm holding on.'
- 'I can't let this happen.'
- 'There's no alternative: we've got to stay together.'

These are phrases we may hear and use often enough, talking to friends or colleagues or neighbours. They show many of the attitudes people have, when they choose to hang on. Some people hang on to failing relationships for years, even decades, and no one can criticize them: only they know what is really going on. Sometimes, the determination to stay together produces couples who have 'weathered the storms together', and are fulfilled by the shared endeavour. They glow with a deep sense of wisdom about their shared life. And there are others who stick together, and are not happy or fulfilled, but never separate.

For those who do break up, and come to look back on the 'We're OK really' attitudes, it can be deeply puzzling and painful to find that these attitudes and approaches simply failed. For them, there was real wisdom contained in these phrases, but it was not enough to see them through. The wise words did not fit their lives, or match their experience.

We can ask, 'Why?' The instant reaction is to assume that we have failed and that we are inadequate. Yet it may be that the 'wisdom' itself was inadequate. The ideas behind these phrases point to a belief in self-sacrifice, resignation, patience, grim determination, self-control, and a forced optimism. While there is nothing wrong with such virtues, marriage may not be the right place for them. A battlefield perhaps, or surviving a shipwreck, but marriage?

The reason that these virtues on their own may be inappropriate is that marriage is not a battle or a place to survive. Rather, it is a place of love, intimate relationship and mutual nurturing, healing and growth.

The pattern of constant hard struggle and effort may go on for years, even decades. Yet, despite all our efforts, sometimes our attempts to 'control' the situation, 'make it work' or 'make the best of it', tend only to make things worse, and we are left with the sad realization that our best efforts have failed. There may have been too much controlling, too many dogmatic rules, and not enough listening. Even well-meaning efforts to change our habits of thinking and feeling, after 'bad patches', may simply make matters worse.

The snag is that self-control can so easily become controlling others. Resignation becomes a mean-hearted grabbing for what is 'mine'. Self-sacrifice becomes a martyred self-pity. Patience becomes 'biding my time' and storing up resentment. Determination is grim because feelings get squashed and blanked out. Optimism is forced because real feelings are left out of the equation.

When I see it like this, the 'wise phrases' become a cover for some pretty murky feelings—most of them quite unhealthy for a close and intimate partnership. If these phrases are all that our culture, society and education have to offer us, to get us through the difficult periods in our relationships, it is not surprising that we come to a point of breakdown. What if the list of wise sayings looked more like this?

- 'I can be honest.'
- 'I will say, or let you see, what I am feeling.'
- 'I will listen carefully and try to accept you.'
- 'I will check to make sure I've heard correctly.'

Before the Break-up

- 'I will respect your point of view.'
- 'I can negotiate openly, and will put my cards on the table.'
- 'I will try to know what I really need and say it.'
- 'I will share my joy with you.'
- 'I will prize and treasure you.'
- 'I will make communication my Number One priority.'
- 'We can thrive, because love is about pain as well as joy.'
- 'I may be angry if I need to be, but I will also be open to hearing what you say.'
- 'I will try to connect with you. I will try never to back off or withdraw.'

This may challenge some of the values and beliefs we have come across as 'received wisdom' in general conversation. Yet there is a profound need for a new look at what helps, and does not help, intimate relationships.

Beginning the Break-up

The following sketch indicates the end of the 'controlled' phase of the relationship, and the initial reaction when the break-up is under way and you know in your heart that there is no other way out. You may well feel reduced in every way, to a wounded state, without power or control over anything, especially yourself. This is not entirely true, but it seems true at the time.

- 'What is happening to us?'
- 'Why is he/she doing this to me?'
- 'This is just a bad dream, it can't be real.'
- 'I cannot bear it.'
- 'I don't deserve this.'
- 'I can't believe he/she is doing this. It's not like him/her.'
- 'My whole life is destroyed.'
- 'I don't understand him/her any more. I thought I did.'
- 'I just can't believe it.'

If you found yourself thinking any of these thoughts, at the start of your break-up, you were not alone. The shock is stunning. How did you find out something was wrong? Did you receive a hard-hearted phone call, or an impersonal letter, have a blazing row or hear from a so-called friend, who just 'had' to tell you? Was an intermediary, a go-between, or even a solicitor involved?

Or did you piece it all together, bit by bit as weeks or months went by? Did you experience sadness, then suspicion and then desolation? Or did you just come home one day, at an unexpected time, and find 'something going on'?

Nothing can prepare anyone for the shock and the trauma. Everything may seem to be felt at once: shock, pain, anger, passion, possessiveness, loss, desire, betrayal, desolation and bereavement. Huge feelings of distrust are common, even of the good times. When so many emotions come simultaneously, the effect is frightening. We are used to coping with emotions that come one at a time: love, happiness, desire, anger, loneliness or joy. But what is so shattering is the onset of so many emotions at once—and the sense that years of meaningful, shared closeness have suddenly been undermined, their meaning stolen and your years of goodwill thrown in the rubbish bin.

It may feel like a primitive, uncivilized state where you are pushed beyond your limits and thrown into some sort of wilderness, where only the most primitive energies for survival will get you through. There may be a terror that you will lose your way in this wilderness, and become something non-human, a 'monster from the swamp'. You imagine that your more delicate feelings, like tenderness and calm, have been crushed for ever, to be replaced by a raging anger or a bottomless sadness.

Ordinary reality may become unreal. Chats with neighbours and friends feel meaningless. Going shopping is a major ordeal. Planning your day more than a few minutes ahead is totally impossible. Even your children seem like ghosts. Parents and good friends suddenly speak a different language. You are on your own, and the world seems to be an alien place.

There may be a sense of appalling threat, as all your assumptions are challenged. Everything you believed in is suddenly worthless. You feel like a complete fool in every way: you made a personal choice and it seems you were wrong. You made a statement about you to the world, and the whole world can see just how wrong you were. You put your faith in someone, and it was totally misplaced. You gave years of your life to a relationship that has been flushed down the pan. You did your best to do what you felt was right, and the signposts you used (religious, parental, social) have led you into a blind alley.

What Might Help?

What might help, in this state of total shock and disorientation? Strangely enough, a routine of some sort can stabilize you. Getting ready for work, forcing yourself to get away on time and be somewhere else, can give some structure to the day when everything else seems to be cracking apart all around you. And when you suspect that you might fall apart too. This does not mean that you should force yourself to drive, or carry out dangerous jobs, when you are feeling slightly crazy, deprived of sleep, or emotionally tormented. But a structure imposed from outside can, sometimes, help when you feel in turmoil inwardly.

Talking to others is a good way of letting off steam and finding support. It helps to choose people you trust, and who are not part of that circle of friends who only know you as part of a couple. If you have been married or partnered for a long time, this may not be easy! But let people know that you need support, and you may be surprised at who comes looking to give it.

Taking care of your children, and concentrating on building real and whole-hearted relationships with them, is another fascinating and emotionally absorbing way of making sense of life. Children are deeply sensitive to any expression of your love and concern, and will show the same love and concern for you.

Beginning the Break-up

A good adviser may work wonders. A priest, experienced in pastoral care, or a counsellor or therapist, may be able to give solid support when you need it most. This is someone who can accept your emotional turmoil without feeling the need to fix your problems, dictate what you should do, or judge you.

Legal advice, if your situation becomes tangled, is essential; though of course, if you can make mediation work to bring about an agreement, there may be no need for the law.

You may need a shoulder to cry on. Sometimes this can be found in unexpected places, when someone reveals that they have been through something similar, and can respond to you from the heart. You are not weak when you show your need for support, quite the opposite! Knowing when you are too full of pain to hold everything together on your own, is a sign of strength.

Steady physical activity can help: digging, swimming, or going for long walks. Look for calm places where your spirit can find its own level, and listen to its own wisdom. Everyone else's wisdom will be out of reach, if your own inner voice is not being heard.

The Egg of Darkness

There is a phase of cold terror that strikes, as the first shock gives way to a numbing realization of what is happening. This is a moment of deep crisis, as all your worst fears are realized. The feelings may come like this:

1. 'Everything seems dark and meaningless.'
2. 'Nothing is worthwhile.'
3. 'He/she has taken everything.'
4. 'Everything has gone dark.'
5. 'My trust is shattered.'
6. 'I have no hope.'
7. 'Everything good has turned to bad.'
8. 'I will hate him/her for ever.'
9. 'How will I cope?'
10. 'Nothing is left.'
11. 'I am worthless.'
12. 'This is insane. It's a disaster.'
13. 'I am bound to die.'
14. 'There is nothing to live for.'

You can brood on this 'egg of darkness', and it may well hatch out! Or you can live with these feelings, allow them to exist, and not be taken over by them. (Relaxation exercises, to focus and hold your feelings and make you aware of your deeper and wider self, have been found helpful in this endeavour.) Then you will gradually come to focus on the implications for your life ahead, not on what is past.

How to do this? Give yourself time. This despair is happening in you now, but it will not last for ever. You may feel paralysed, but this is part of a natural reaction to trauma. You have suffered a severe shock, but you can come through this.

There is no need to deny, or gloss over, these feelings. There is no need to pretend you are made of stone, or can bounce back into fun and laughter instantly. Be gentle with yourself. This darkness can be a gateway into a new state of awareness about yourself. Optimism and peacefulness may lie at the other end, but your journey is in a dark place at the moment. Consider the following, which are direct challenges to the attitudes contained in the statements above.

Counter-truths

1. I am worthwhile: no matter what has happened to me, I have something to do in life that only I can do. I am unique, and my contribution is unique.

2. My life is worthwhile. Everything around me is valuable, because I am here to give it value. I have light and love in me, and I need to let that show.

3. I have all I really need: me! If I can believe in me, I can cope with whatever life throws at me.

4. I did believe in the old certainties once, and they have had their day. I am wiser now. I don't need to be stuck in the old patterns and expectations.

5. I am building a new kind of trust: I don't need the old way of trusting.

6. I have a new kind of hope: one that is centred in me and my worth, rather than on expectations about other people, and dependency on them.

7. The old reality has gone. Perhaps something beautiful has died, has run its course. But it has died to make way for something else, perhaps differently beautiful.

8. I feel crazy now, lost and disorientated. But the past was insane in its own way: I could not have gone on like that. There was something unreal about it.

9. I will cope, and more than cope. How will I be truly me? The possibilities are endless! How shall I make a start? How can I start to know what I alone have to do?

10. I need to take very little with me from the old relationship: just myself. Out of that, I can make anything.

11. Loving me is the key to loving anyone else—even the person who has hurt me most. I am finding out my true worth, my own way of being and loving.

12. The light has gone out of the old relationship, but it has reappeared in me on my own. It's the beginning of a new beginning.

13. If Christian, my faith tells me I am made in God's likeness. The glory that is in me cannot be taken away.

The Egg of Darkness

14. Something has died, for ever. Something new has been born.

No one can tell you to believe these things, but they may help in making the dark times more comprehensible and bearable.

The False Dawn

In the agony of darkness and loss of hope, you may go through a phase of rebellion and denial. You may feel surges of disbelief, of powerful hope that this *cannot be real*, and that *something must be done* to roll back what has happened. It may be that the thoughts and feelings look like the following:

1. 'This cannot be the end.'
2. 'I'll get him/her back.'
3. 'It's all right really.'
4. 'We can talk it through.'
5. 'He/she will come to their senses.'
6. 'I'll fight every step of the way.'
7. 'I'll do anything to get him/her back.'
8. 'This is just some silly game.'
9. 'It's a passing infatuation: he/she will see reason.'
10. 'I've only got to "hang on in" there.'

This is another set of reactions, that could be denying what is happening and trying to get back to the old certainties of the relationship, whatever they were. These phrases can be part of a rebellious reaction, an urge to have 'one last go' in the face of overwhelming odds. It is important that your actions at this time do not become a futile waste of energy and time, a forlorn gesture that only creates further damage. The counter-truths are complex but real.

Counter-truths

1. 'This cannot be the end.' Denying the end is almost guaranteed to make the whole process longer and more painful. Denial is a well-recognized phase, and happens at the start of (or during) many people's experiences of shock, loss and trauma. In this type of ending, you will eventually know that this can indeed be the end, and that you need not resist: but it is the end of the relationship, not you.

2. 'I'll get him/her back.' You may indeed 'get someone back', but it is very unlikely, and even if you do, the relationship will probably never be what it once was. When the situation has come right to the point of breaking up, the 'leaver' has already done lots of thinking and preparation, and (most important) has disengaged from you emotionally. He or she is more like a shadow or a ghost than a real person. Attempts to hurt just seem to pass straight through! And attempts to pull them back fail for the same reason. They are just not there any more.

The False Dawn

3. 'It's all right really.' *You* are all right, or will be. Your life will come to make sense one day. The relationship is not all right, and probably has not been all right for many years. It is anxiety in you that insists it is OK—an effort to make it OK by insisting that it is. This is a kind of 'wishing' reaction—if I say it enough, wish it enough, it will come true.

4. 'We can talk it through.' Talking will not bring anything back, once one partner has made the break. Talking will clarify the best way to go from here, but can never turn back the clock. The time for talking has passed.

5. 'He/she will come to their senses.' Only *you* can come to *your* senses. You can only make your own efforts yourself. It is simpler, and happier, that way! It sounds a bit childish to say it like this, but how many of us try desperately to make other people think, feel and act in just the way we would, not seeing the giant hurdles they would have to leap across to get there? In concentrating on what makes sense for you alone, you gain your own power of self-respect, not dependent on what anyone else says or does.

6. 'I'll fight every step of the way.' Fighting can only be done within yourself, if it is to be productive. You may honourably fight the demons within yourself, the dragons of jealousy or revenge or destructiveness. You may fight to protect your inner dignity and loving nature. In this way, your inner strength and wisdom are increased. To fight someone outside you, for mastery in some battle, is at best a short-term and limited strategy. For you to be destructive during the aftermath of separation, in negotiations about property, or time with the children, or money, is to run the risk of creating even more pain and difficulty in the future. In return for a fleeting sense of satisfaction, you have made the whole process longer, reduced your ability to take pride in yourself, and opened up new wounds.

7. 'I'll do anything to get him/her back.' Like famous King Canute, this one is bound to fail. You cannot turn back the clock, any more than Canute could turn back the tide. He or she is unlikely to turn back, once set on a course that has probably been thought through for many weeks and months. Pleading, tears, and desperate gestures will simply seem repellent and bizarre, if his or her emotions have been shut down, and the attachment and loyalty to you given to someone else, or simply terminated.

8. 'This is just some silly game.' It is likely that you may both have been trapped in some 'silly game' for years. However it started, and however much one or both partners feel hard done by, the cold truth is that it 'takes two to tango'. The relationship has probably been set on this course for years, and at some time in

The False Dawn

the future you will look back and take pity on the two people who were lost in that maze. There is more sadness than silliness in all of it.

9. 'It's a passing infatuation: he/she will see reason.' It is hard to judge what is infatuation in another person. The affair may have all the hallmarks of being short-term, selfish and pointless, yet it may last; whereas your marriage, built on goodwill and idealism, sinks. There is no way to make the judgement about someone else, even your partner whom you thought you knew so well.

10. 'I've only got to "hang on in" there.' Hang on to yourself! And hang on for yourself! Hanging on to someone else will only drive that person away. Hanging on to hate and fury will only damage you. Try to see your needs and priorities, and hold on to those.

The Estranged World

Another aspect of the separation process is the way that the whole world outside suddenly looks and sounds and feels different. People say things that sound strange, or start to act strangely. There is a sense in which not only is your relationship breaking up, but the world outside is not prepared to listen or to understand. Parents, your social circle, old friends, teachers and people who have supported you in the past—all look at you in a new way.

From close family, you may hear comments that reject your experience, your choices, and your wisdom.
'You've made your bed, now lie in it.'
'I did my best for you but now you are grown up.'
'You never did listen to me.'
'You're really setting a bad example.'
'Your brothers and sisters might get ideas, if you divorce.'
'What will it do to Grandma or Grandad?'

From your social circle, and even from those who share your religious faith and church membership, you may feel the same sense of judgement and rejection.
'I don't know what to think.'
'I wouldn't know what to say.'
'They would give us a bad name.'
'You've broken your vows.'
'Get some help from the priest.'
'You'd be better off in a different church, not this one.'

Friends in the neighbourhood and community may react with their own sense of disbelief and worry.
'I can't believe they've split up.'
'They always seemed so happy.'
'What are they doing to/with their children?'
'I always thought he/she was too good to be true.'
'All their airs and graces ... now look at them.'
'They never did really belong round here.'

There may be a confused sense of being threatened by your new single status and the assumed effects on other marriage partners, and on the children of existing marriages. People may feel forced to take sides, where many couples all know each other.

'They have let the side down.'
'We can't have him/her round here.'
'The children will feel awkward.'
'We used to have you round … but now it's so awkward.'
'I suppose he/she will be round here every minute.'
'I don't want her sort messing with my husband.'

One of the wounding and, perhaps, unexpected aspects of a partnership breakdown is the way that it affects the whole social web consisting of friends, other couples, the parents of your children's friends, and neighbourhood acquaintances. The whole balance of the network is forced to change, because your relationship is breaking up.

In your very vulnerable state, you will be very hurt when some people, who you thought were good friends, suddenly withdraw. They are hard to speak to, distant in what they say, and you never seem to see them any more. You will sense that some friends and couples are becoming polarized, forced to choose between you and your ex-partner. You may know that there is no need to choose between you, but they may not see it that way. Even if they decide not to choose between you, they may well withdraw from both of you, feeling baffled by the whole situation.

Many couples may find your decision extremely threatening to their own partnership or marriage. If you, who appeared to be so solid and dependable, can break up, then it could happen to them also. In an almost superstitious way, they may not want you around. You may even find that your new status as 'single' or 'unattached' makes you a threat: they were close to you as part of a couple but, on your own, you suddenly become a threat. It is a very human response, but it may hurt profoundly, when the last thing on your mind is to find someone else!

The most painful comments may come from old friends who just cannot believe what has happened to you: 'I remember you both in the old days: what went wrong?' That is the question that may be tormenting you, too, and at this early phase of the break-up, you do not have any clear answers either. Being asked the question just seems to open all the wounds yet again.

Counter-truths

There is very little that can be done to change anybody's reaction to your break-up. People will be thrown back onto their own ideas, judgements, and fears. Your social network will change, and you may be shocked at how some former friends can judge you or disown you. Sadly, that may also apply to relatives and even to parents.

The Estranged World

On the other hand, there will be people who suddenly become very supportive and warm. People who were only slight friends become very close, or lend a hand just when you need it, or say just the right thing. Others who have been through something similar will lend their advice and insights. You suddenly discover a whole new network of people with experience and understanding, and their wisdom can be crucial while you find your feet, in the most painful moments of your separation process. Sometimes, people where you work, or in the corner shop, or at the crèche, will suddenly reveal that they themselves have been through this. You will find support where you least expect it, and usually it will come with no strings attached. Your need will be just to get through, one day at a time, and contacts like these will be beyond price: just a loving word, and a simple offer, will make all the difference.

Looking Back to Look Forwards

Looking back on what happened, it is often stunningly clear after the event. But before the break-up, everything looked different. How can it be so different?

Amid the shock and pain of breaking up will come many moments—perhaps in the long hours of the night—when you may find yourself asking, 'What really happened?' You will search for the signs that could have given you early warning of what was coming, and for the pointers to what was really happening at the time. The point of looking at these signs and pointers is not to brood endlessly, or dredge up the pain, or dish out blame. The point is to get some clarity on exactly what happened, who did what, who contributed, and how much, what the motives were, and whose needs or agendas were being met.

It is important to get this clarity, otherwise you can feel you are going insane. You may find yourself plagued with questions. Was it all your fault? Were you blind all the time? How could you be so stupid? Such questions only increase your distress, and well-meaning friends can be accidentally unhelpful, when they try to make out that all the blame lies with your ex-partner. In your heart of hearts, you know it is not a black-and-white picture. Nothing was clear-cut. In the end, you need realism more than you need sympathy. There are difficult, grown-up decisions to take, and painful choices to put into action. Looking back is an essential part of being ready for the future.

The need to know exactly what went on is your need to find out what part you played in it all, both deliberately and, more mysteriously, without knowing what you were doing. This may include the motives you did not see in yourself; things you said which you did not really mean; games you played that were not real; and positions you got into which were never part of your original intention. All of this is hard to admit to yourself, yet this is precisely where you need the clarity most.

It has to be said that you are unlikely to get much help: friends and other helpers may find that helping you to open up these difficult issues often exposes them to asking the same questions about their own lives. They would rather not be part of anything that might expose their own compromises, unhappiness, or false positions. They will tend to leave you well alone if you are trying to go down the path of understanding yourself better.

Looking Back to Look Forwards

The need to carry out this inner work of understanding yourself is not just important for your present mental and emotional well-being. It is important for the future. One day, though it may be hard to believe it when the pain is at its worst, you will quite likely find yourself making choices about a new relationship, deciding whether you are able to put yourself into closeness and intimacy with a new partner. It is then that the chips will be down, and the real questions will come up. Have you seen clearly what you did in the last relationship, or at least some of it? Have you accepted your part in it (and only your part!) and are you ready to risk everything again, knowing what happened last time?

Breakdown in Communication

You may find it helpful to look at the relationship in terms of its communication pattern. Vulnerability in intimate relationship, defensiveness and shutting down, and leading parallel lives, may combine to cause an on-going breakdown in communication.

Vulnerability

For most people, the intimacy of an intense, committed relationship is both exciting and intimidating. You are so close to someone else, and they know everything about you—or nearly everything. There are sides to you which you may not be ready to reveal, and which you may never reveal, and never need to. But the intimacy is still intense, and the sense of being exposed and vulnerable is equally strong.

Looking back, you may remember times when you had something to say but could not speak. This can be a permanent feature of many relationships! You may recall inability or unwillingness to speak; a feeling of being unsupported or unsafe; feeling shut off, or out of touch; and being aware of resentments which were never expressed. Perhaps you are not too sure what it was, exactly, that you might have wanted to say, but you might have spoken, if the atmosphere had been right. In fact, the atmosphere was not right, and you did not, could not, speak. This is a situation where both partners feel so vulnerable that things cannot be said.

Shutting Down

It is easy to feel shut off and out of touch, once sensitive areas are touched on. Arguments and disagreements tend to end up in these sensitive areas, even when they are not in fact the central concern. People can end up feeling very hurt and injured. Words have been said, and cannot be taken back. The whole area is a 'minefield', and neither partner wants to open it up again, because each feels so vulnerable. Arguments turn into rows. People begin to react defensively even before a word has been spoken, and then to attack with wounding words. Co-operation and respect disappear. 'You're always like this!' Arguments and rows, serious disagreements, unresolved hurts and injuries, and a dogged sense of resignation may have built up within the relationship. The result is that matters are no longer discussed. Resentments are not spoken, even when they are justified. 'You could have phoned to say you were leaving late!' There is a sense of resignation in one or both: 'I suppose this is the best we can do', 'No good wishing for what is not possible'. And all the time something inside is wishing for precisely that, and it may be that both of you have been feeling the same but dare not speak. After the separation, there is no way of knowing, because it is too late to find out.

This feeling of being unsafe, misunderstood, or unsupported, is a key factor in many communication breakdowns. From the one 'sensitive' subject, a kind of infection spreads to other things. There is fear involved, between the two people, and it feeds on itself. A huge tower of silence and misunderstanding is built on simple foundations: 'We had better not open that up again! It always causes a row.' The result is a shutting down of communication.

Parallel Lives

A couple can begin living parallel lives, feeling shut into their own routines and chores, and shut out of their partner's life. It begins to be easy to get out of touch: 'I didn't know you had to go out tonight!' They become more distant, lose the sense of intimacy, and the sparkle goes out of the relationship. Sex may go out of the window altogether, or become a short, perfunctory encounter, lacking any sort of emotional depth. The sense of not being appreciated becomes deeper: 'You used me and then threw me away' or 'I was never good enough for you'. Physically, the couple are in the same space less and less, as one may be out at work all the time, and the other makes sure they have plenty to do in the evenings. The silence continues to grow.

Finally, there are the outright deceptions and dishonesty, which often come at the end of a long period of mistrust and silence. They include simple but deliberate unreliability, like not being where you said you would be; making friendships that are unhelpful to your relationship; affairs and adultery; squandering or gambling away the family money, and deliberately hurtful actions and words. Such hurts and injuries will be carried for ever: 'You betrayed my trust: how can I ever trust anyone again?'

Building a New Picture of Yourself

I am not trying to make excuses for any of this behaviour. The point is not that everyone is to blame, or that no one is to blame. I am suggesting that, behind every simple story, there is a complicated web to disentangle, and that only you

Looking Back to Look Forwards

can really say what you did or did not do. I am also suggesting that the way you figure out what happened can only be a hypothesis, a theory that will be tested later, again and again. Instead of making judgements like 'I always knew he/she was a rat', you can gently probe what went on, trying to build up a different picture from the one you saw at the time. When you see more clearly what happened, you will also see yourself differently, and this is the purpose of the whole exercise. When you are equipped with a different view of yourself in the past, you can give yourself the freedom to be different in the future.

Along the way, there will be moments of deep pain and distress, as you suddenly understand his or her words differently, and see the meaning that was invisible at the time. This is a poignant, painful task. There is so much of the feeling, 'If only I had responded differently, if I had just seen what he/she meant!' I remember vividly a time when my first wife said, as I left to go on duty at a telephone helpline, 'You're going out to listen to other people's problems, but mine are far worse than theirs'. I never asked what she meant, because we were not communicating very well then. I took it as a vague threat. Three years later, we separated.

I know that there was little I could have done at the time: I was different then, and unable to see what I was doing to make her so lonely. Now I can see it, and I regret it, but many years have gone by since then and I am in a new life. It could be that, whatever I might have done differently, it would have made no difference in the end. I will never know, but I will keep that moment in mind, testing my behaviour now, in a different relationship, to make sure that I am never so blind again.

This 'second sight' picture which you build up will always be provisional. Unlike the certainty of love and passion the first time round, where everything seems so right and everlasting, this second view of what went on will always contain the thought, 'I could have done it differently,' as well as the question, 'Could I really have been different?' There are no easy answers, and it is OK to live with two truths at the same time. You will feel more flexible about responding to challenges if you do!

Knowing yourself better is crucial to being different next time round, because this will involve developing new facets of your personality. Nothing is the same twice, and you need to know where you are starting from, to chart your course into the future. In a later chapter, I will look at using angry energy as a way of cutting the ties with the past, and taking purposeful steps towards your own future. This short exploration around self-awareness represents the first step towards that more dynamic engagement with your own potential.

The Wilderness Choice

The One Who Leaves

What happens if you are the one doing the leaving? I have written so far from a perspective dominated by the feelings of the ones who *are left*, rather than the ones who *do the leaving*. I believe that there is a marked difference between the two at the time of the announcement of the separation. One person usually feels that he/she has been hit by a bolt from the blue. The other has planned it carefully, or at least has some idea in advance of what he/she will say. Perhaps the mere fact of being the one who is actively doing something makes the actual announcement a lot easier. But I do not believe that the one doing the leaving is not suffering, or has not spent many hours, days or months in agonizing about finally making the move. There are usually deep, powerful, and irresistible feelings involved in making such a profoundly important decision. It is my belief that no one wants to cause someone else this much pain! Or at least, causing pain is not the primary motive.

The thoughts of the one leaving may fall into one of several categories, depending on the motives for leaving. Those motives may be multiple and complex. From the outside, the 'reason' may seem simple. 'She left me for someone else.' 'He didn't like being tied down.' 'She just wanted my money.' But, from the inside, there may be confusion, mixed feelings, and panic. The urge to get away may be powerful, but so is loyalty to the marriage and an unwillingness to hurt. There may be shame about how you will seem to others, especially if you expect to be 'cold-shouldered' by them. You may suspect, with good reason, that they will judge you, and you will never be allowed to tell your side of the story.
'I can't believe I'm doing this.'
'I don't want to let anyone down, but I have no choice.'
'I'm going into unknown territory.'
'I've found someone who understands, who really listens.'
'No one knows what I've been through.'
'I'm so sorry for all the pain that he/she will feel.'

It may be that you just need a break from the pressures and restrictions. The marriage may seem like one long list of demands, chores, and drudgery. You feel that someone has taken you for granted, taken everything you could give, and is having the easy part of the bargain. You like the feeling of finding someone who makes you feel good, gives you a bit of pride in yourself, and makes life sparkle.
'So this is what it's like to be unfaithful.'

The Wilderness Choice

'Something for me at last.'
'I deserve this: it's something different, just a break, a bit of fun.'
'I need to get away.'
'Anything would be better than this.'
'I can't stand it any more.'

The reason for leaving may be deadly serious: a situation of threat, abuse or violence. Your feelings may be battered as much as your body. Your will to escape may be paper-thin, but the thought of leaving may be all that keeps you alive. Even in this desperate state, the attempt to be fair and even-handed may still be important.

'He/she has got this coming.'
'I'm breaking out at last.'
'I'm only taking what is mine.'

You may have chosen to leave from a feeling of intense depression. Your feelings may be confused and meaningless, even to yourself. There is just an overwhelming need to get away, to escape, and be yourself in a safe place. There are no reasons or justifications: you will do your best not to be hurtful, but if you do not get away you will go mad—or worse. The sense of threat and impotence within the relationship is worse than anything you could meet outside.

'I'm trapped, doing my best for everyone.'
'I'm waiting … until the right moment.'
'I'm frightened but I'm still going.'
'This is the worst moment of my life.'
'This is my hardest choice ever.'
'I am fated to make this choice: I have no choice.'

Whatever the reasons, the one leaving has generally planned well in advance. The emotional crisis has happened much earlier than the actual separation, and there is a coolness about the leaving when it happens. However, leaving will always be a painful memory, as guilt and self-blame arise unexpectedly. Small things, like anniversaries and birthdays, can stay emotionally charged for years afterwards.

When a Woman Leaves

Our social stereotypes lead us to suspect that the one breaking up the family unit by leaving will be the man. Our moral condemnation is centred around the stereotype of the woman and child (or children) who need the man's protection. Society traditionally condemns fathers who leave, despite the fact that most divorces are initiated by women. However, in the case where it is the mother who leaves, society tends to be even more unfeeling and condemnatory. The two personal testimonies that follow unfold a woman's point of view. Through them I am trying to widen our understanding by challenging the stereotypes around mothers and children. Real life is much more complex than these stereotypes will allow.

Sophie's Story

I was divorced four years ago from a relationship of ten years. The process of painful separation on my part started long before divorce. When we first met we felt so strong, so certain, so 'for each other'. I was proud of him and he of me. He was ambitious, we had dreams of amazing family life—what we could create together. He valued loyalty, I valued communication. Before we married, the cracks and gaps in our communication process were beginning to show.

After having one child, I was working and not coping. He had started an additional course as well as his full-time degree, and he was working. We had agreed that if things got too much then he would suspend the additional course. Things got too much for me. He continued with his courses. I felt unheard. He felt unsupported. Things were good enough to continue. I did not know what else to do. I think he had a vision for the future. I lost mine.

I had another child, this time at home. I was still trying to create a family, to hold myself together, to meet the needs of the children. I felt I was tearing apart. At the same time, I was taking initiatives for myself. I went on an assertiveness course. I went on a co-counselling course. We were now moving in diverging directions. I felt like a single parent. I started behaving more like one. I had little sense of the impact of my behaviour on him or maybe I did—I wanted to impact on him and I could not see or feel a response. There was tension in the air. I was making contacts, friends. I was reaching out. I got a therapist. I did superficial work but it got me along. We were both clinging to a distant dream still. We moved house. I felt as if I was on holiday, going to go home very soon. I could not settle. The plants died. I was desperate. I was drowning. I got another therapist. I felt held, heard. The power of my drive to leave was greater than the power of my clinging. I let go.

At first all seemed quiet. I started living for half the week in a rented room and went back at the end of the week to care for our children. When I left with my things, he was watching the rugby and cheering with the scores. I was numb. We said that I would move out for part of the time and after six months decide whether I was to move back in or move out totally. Once I had gone, though, that was it. I could not return. I had some space, some control, some sense of freedom.

The separation from my children was painful. I was in agony. I felt a terrible uncertainty about the future. But I trusted him to be caring enough. I thought we would be able to work through to a solution 'like adults', rationally.

I bought a house. I was feeling more stable. I was wanting, and available for, more time with my children. They wanted more time with me. My husband said I could not see them any more than I was already seeing them. I went cold.

In the spirit of us 'working things out together' we had both visited a solicitor of his choosing to work out a 'separation agreement' so that we knew where we both stood in relation to our responsibilities, assets, debts, and the children. At the time we agreed that our children would live in our marital home while I arranged for somewhere to live and was putting my energy into getting paid work to support myself and my children. We agreed, and it was detailed that the situation would be reviewed regularly as our needs changed.

When I was more stable, the fragile communication that had existed went cold. I no longer experienced us working together at all. We became adversaries. He began to make decisions about the children with his new partner and did not inform me. They chose a new school for them. He assumed control of their contact with me.

I felt disbelieving, cold, speechless, and terrified. Things happened fast then. He wanted a divorce. He wanted to divorce me for adultery. I felt smacked by injustice, winded. He said that I had signed the children over to him, that I was only their biological mother.

I wanted to be angry. I was mainly grief-stricken, sadness to the core, I was so racked with it. I was terrified that ultimately I would be denied contact with my children. He divorced me for 'unreasonable behaviour'. I had lost a relationship. There was hate and fear and grief between us. I desperately wanted to foster my understanding of him and his of me (mainly his of me). I thought I could understand why he was behaving the way he was. I stopped trying so hard to make it better. I focused on arguing my case and standing my ground with warmth and understanding put aside. It was straight, determined negotiating.

I was most angry with his hypocrisy over their religious upbringing—his insistence that his values were right and should dominate. I felt outraged when the court process was prolonged. He wanted to take the children to church every Sunday and that meant taking them out of my care for a morning. The values we held seemingly could not be held alongside each other. His insistence on righteousness felt outrageous, absurd to me. The message I continued to receive was that it was more important for them to go to church than to have time with me. He clearly did not value our children's relationship with me through all our negotiations. That hurt. There was definitely an abuse of power. Court support, the cost of pursuing the money that was mine, was too much. I let it go. (Sometimes it tugs.) I got what was important, i.e. myself, and secured a court-written document defining contact with my children. It's only up and out from here!

Regrets? I could not have done it differently at the time. I managed the absolute best that I could. It was as it was. It is as it is. I think that we both did the best we could.

I am in a better place now. Seismic change! My world view has changed enormously. I trust myself more, am clearer about my own values and value. I have a sense of identity now, a sense of self-growing. I am less deluded. I have more sense of personal responsibility. I have self-esteem as a person and as a mother. I am valuable. I am lovable. I can be free and be in relationship. Wow! I can be separate and loved!

What has the experience given me? Birth by fire! I burned, I trembled and I survived stronger. I feel. I can respond. I have choice. I can be supported. I can look after myself. I will not die because I am not in relationship. I can be separate. I can be separate and in relationship. I can grow. I can say what I want, what I need. I will be heard by some and not by others. I am unique. I can be different and not 'wrong'. I can find support. I have a depth of understanding of deep grief. I have self-security to venture into painful worlds without anxiety of fragmentation, disappearance or panic. I have self-anchorage. I have containment and holding of self and therefore of others. I have a sense of resourcefulness when the chips are down: an inner self-confidence as well as boldness, an intolerance of injustice and the will to model change.

Alice's Story

The break-up of my first marriage was twenty years ago. I feel that it was initiated by the fact that we grew apart. I married quite young. My first child was born when I was nearly twenty and not really ready for the responsibility of motherhood.

My husband worked away from home for some of the time and I felt quite isolated living on a new housing estate with very few friends in the area. At the time I was unable to drive. I gradually made friends in the area and after my second child had started school I began a course of further education. This seemed to open up a new circle of friends for me, and an opportunity to work outside the home. This caused some resentment between my husband and me and gradually the marriage began to break down.

I was now in full-time work and enjoying my job but also having to take on the responsibility of being both mother and father to the children due to my husband's work commitments. I began to feel that I was almost like a single parent. Also throughout the marriage I had been the one to take on the responsibility for ensuring that the bills were paid on time and that the financial aspect was in order.

Realizing that neither my husband nor I was happy in the relationship, and that the children were not particularly happy, I suggested that, if we moved house and made a fresh start, things might work out. My partner was not happy to do this. I decided that I wanted a divorce and, although I felt scared, I felt I had to go through with it.

The things that made me most fearful were the court proceedings that I had to go through. I felt like a criminal, and that solicitors were manipulating me into compromises that I did not want to make. I was also fearful because my eldest son had to choose with whom he wanted to live. At the time he chose his father, which split the family even more, as I had one son and my husband had my other son. This caused great difficulties, and I did not see my elder son for some time.

The result of all this is that our family relationships are extremely difficult. My elder son does not have contact with his brother or me. Also my elder son refuses me access to his daughter, my granddaughter.

There have been times when I have felt extremely low. I have been on the verge of having an eating disorder but somehow for the sake of my family I have found an inner strength, or some kind of survival instinct, which has enabled me to carry on and also to help others in a similar situation.

I feel the experience is part of the grief and loss process, but in some ways more complicated because my ex-husband is still alive although I am not part of his life any more, and I know that he is living a different life somewhere else.

Thoughts on How we Judge

The urge to judge or condemn those who leave a marriage may be strong. Politicians, church people, and those with an axe to grind may be involved in whipping up an atmosphere of hysteria about marriage and family breakdown. In challenging the stereotypes of who leaves a marriage or partnership, and why, I am also exploring how we make choices and judgements.

It is important to see that each breakdown is complex and unique: the couple is unique, and so is their relationship. We all have choices to make, and each person makes the deepest choices alone. No dogmatic statement can override the freedom to choose of any individual human being, and there is no single law that can cover all the complicated situations in which people find themselves.

A principle may guide the choice you make but, in the end, your conscience is able to turn away from dogmatic truths and inflexible pronouncements. The only practical application of a principle is in the light of the unique circumstances that surround it. The only productive way to see the meaning of a breakdown is in the light of love: a respect for the individuals involved, a concern for their complete well-being, and sensitivity to their special circumstances. We would not wish anything less for ourselves!

The urge to judge others is especially strong around marriage. It is an 'institution' like no other for, in a marriage, the individual private and personal world meets social reality, the political and economic factors which bear on marriages, community expectations, and religious beliefs. We can all take up a stance on any one of these grounds. Further, we have all been in close relationships, even if only in childhood, and feel that we have solid experience of what must be true. Hence the tendency to make judgements is increased and reinforced. I hope that the stories in this chapter and in other parts of the book will reinforce my contention that what matters is the reality and complexity of people's actual lives, and our ability to promote love and acceptance for all, throughout the process of breaking up.

Violence Against Women

Some women are forced to leave relationships because of violence. The problem of violence against women is too important, and too neglected, to be glossed over here. While men are not free from abuse, it is overwhelmingly men who abuse women. Women leave relationships because of violence, whether physical, sexual, or emotional. The facts are not widely recognized. Each week, two women are killed by their current or former partners.

Violence to women from men they know involves the abuse of power and control. The violence or abuse can be physical, sexual, emotional or psychological, or any combination of these, and can include racism and other forms of oppression to maintain control. The effects on women suffering violence from men they know are tremendous. Here are some.

- Women often live in fear and under constant threat of violence. They may be embarrassed by their situation and unable to tell someone what is happening to them.

The Wilderness Choice

- Women are often isolated from friends and family, and they may be kept financially dependent by the perpetrator.

- Women may blame themselves for their situation—perpetrators often shift the blame for their violence onto the women.

- Women can become emotionally disabled by the violence and abuse, with the result that they suffer from depression and/or 'stress-related illnesses'. Illnesses such as these can impact on women's ability to function, which in turn can affect their ability to meet their own and their children's needs.

- Mothers often feel guilt about the situation in which they and their children have to live. They may find it hard to discuss the violence with their children.

- Women can lack self-confidence as women and as mothers, as a result of violence.

- The perpetrator may use children to abuse their own mothers.

- Women may be afraid to seek help, fearing that their children will be taken away from them. They are also afraid that they will not be believed.

- In addition to feeling guilt, they feel failure and shame at being in the situation. Cultural and religious expectations on women can further reduce their ability to seek and find help.

Many women feel trapped in their situation. Sometimes this can be a physical reality, where the perpetrator is actually keeping them prisoner. Some women are locked in their homes and escorted everywhere by the perpetrator, making it impossible to seek help. Women can be silenced by fear of reprisals. Women's loss of self, and the loss of even their sense of their own humanity, may result in them being unable to make any decisions, whether about themselves or about others.

Racist attitudes make life even worse for black women. When women do seek help, it has been found that, on average, white women will make contact with eleven agencies before they receive help. For black women, this number rises to seventeen. Any marginalized group will experience the same difficulties: black and Asian women, disabled women, older women, traveller women, women working in prostitution, and lesbians will face additional barriers to obtaining the support and advice they need.

To leave any relationship demands a huge amount of energy and emotional strength.

The Wilderness Choice

Women suffering violence are often disabled from leaving. Their whole level of functioning is reduced. There are many reasons why women stay, or are unable to leave.

- Most women have to leave in secrecy to protect their safety. Men often threaten women as a way of keeping them in the relationship. For instance, 'If you leave, I will kill myself'; 'I'll find you and kill you'; 'I'll kill the children'. It is a fact that women are more likely to be killed by their partner once they have left the relationship than when they are still in it.

- Women have few places to go. Information and services may be difficult to access.

- Women may have to leave on the spur of the moment, and may not have time to make arrangements and plans.

- Even if they have managed to plan their escape secretly, they have to cope with problems of transport, and finding someone to help. It is often unsafe to use friends, family or neighbours, as perpetrators can intimidate them or follow them, to find out where the woman has gone. Sometimes, women have to make a clean break with all their previous connections, in order to preserve their safety. It is very rare for a woman to be able to take all her possessions with her: much has to be left behind.

- Finance is a major issue for women. Men often claim benefits for themselves and the woman, meaning the woman has no income in her own right. Working men may keep all the money coming into the household as a means of control. The couple may have incurred debts, and some men make sure that bills and loans are in the woman's name, so that she is responsible for any debts.

- Women may not be aware of their rights and the available options for support in such situations. This ignorance may itself be used by the perpetrator as a means of keeping her in the relationship, by keeping her financially dependent.

- Leaving the relationship can mean that the woman has to accept a lower standard of living. She may be leaving a house that she has worked hard to establish, to go into temporary, shared accommodation, which itself creates added stress. Women can easily experience a loss of status and identity as a result of leaving.

- Women often feel guilty about the impact on the children of leaving. The children may not want to leave. Women may feel guilty of depriving them of their father. Children also have to leave possessions, pets, friends, etc. They will

The Wilderness Choice

probably have to change schools, and may blame their mother for the situation. Keeping their whereabouts secret can be a huge responsibility for children.

- Women may experience pressure from family, friends and the children to stay in the family home.

- There is also the fear of the unknown for women who may find themselves in an unfamiliar town or city, where they feel isolated and alone, living with the fear of being found, and the consequences of that.

Jennie's Story

The break-up came about sixteen years ago, after eighteen years of a very violent marriage. I always knew some day I would divorce him, but he left me for a much older woman.

I was angered by the thought that, after all the violence, he had the nerve to leave me, and that his new partner was over twenty years older than I was. And after three days, he came back and said that he didn't like it where he was—not that he loved me or the kids! Once more, it was all him and his needs.

It took years to come to terms with some of the hurtful things he did. I feel that I will never truly cope with the violent things he did. Rejection, and the feeling of being so stupid, made me hurt so much—and the feeling of being controlled about everything life seems to stand for.

I was afraid of the loneliness, and always feeling I was not coping well with the divorce. I was fearful for the kids. I did know they were going through a bad time, but I feel at times I only saw my needs and not theirs. He did leave me in a lot of debt and I had money worries, but I was most fearful because I had forgotten where 'me' was. I felt lost with no meaning to life any more, and at times could not see any way forward.

Two years after the divorce, I was admitted to a psychiatric unit after I tried to kill myself. I was in the day hospital for about one year. I still feel bad about this, and why I let myself down, and my kids. The kids and my Dad kept me going—my Dad more than anyone because I felt he was the only person who truly loved me. My greatest sources of help came from a very kind nurse, and my kids. The police were useless, and at that time there was no other help.

I have a number of regrets—that, after accepting in court £4.10 each week, I let him get away with paying only once. That I did not make him pay half the bill. That I ever met him and that I did not hit back.

I am in a better place now. After many men in my life, and two long-term failed relationships, I am in a very good relationship now. He is older than I am and I feel that helps because he seems to understand me. We do have problems like all couples, but I always know he will never physically hurt me. And that was always my worry in all relationships after my divorce. I became violent myself to some of the men. I feel I just had to test them all, and that I will never truly let the brick wall down just in case I cannot cope with love and support.

Thank God, today there is help for men and women. I would never have been too proud to ask for help. But for myself, it was a learning process through life. I feel I am a better person for all the pain. I look at my kids, and ask, 'What did I put them through?' I always felt that if I sent them upstairs they would not see or hear anything: how wrong I was! They are grown up now, and we talk about things: we are very close. But the kids tell me things that their Dad is up to and I feel how lucky I am to be me.

The Volcano of Anger

If anger comes as part of your process of dealing with separation or divorce, it can be devastating when it hits you. Out of all the pain and hurt comes a set of feelings that are very difficult to accept and work with. For instance, out of the disbelief and shock may come an urge to protect yourself and your dignity:

'He/she has no right to do this to me.'
'What the hell is going on?'
'I'm not taking this lying down.'

Then there may be a clutching for ways to assert yourself, a sort of grab at the nearest thing that will hurt back.

'I'll screw him/her for everything they've got.'
'I'll take the kids.'
'I'll screw someone else.'

A wild disillusionment may be mixed in with the anger, an exaggerated sense of self as a victim of some cosmic confidence trick.

'There's no such thing as justice.'
'Everything I believed in is just crap.'
'I worked so hard at this, and now look what's happened!'

There may be an urge to set instant boundaries, to set up hasty barricades and mark out what is yours.

'He/she won't get a penny.'
'After all I've done for him/her, all I've put up with and suffered…'
'It's my turn to act selfish now.'

There is often a total mistrust of people, of men or women, a feeling of being totally abandoned and alone.

'They (men, or women) are all liars and cheats.'
'Nobody warned me, nobody said a thing.'
'I can't trust anyone.'

An urge for revenge may also be a feature, and you may be shocked at just how violent the feelings are, or how violent the language is. But the fiery language is not what you actually intend to do: it is just one way of expressing the depth of your hurt and letting go of the pain.

'I'll make him/her suffer, no matter how long it takes.'
'The gloves are off now.'

'I have more hate in me than he/she ever knew.'

These are all emotions that may come as part of the anger at the end of the relationship. The feelings are volcanic in their rawness and intensity. They push their way out, whether you 'allow' them or not. They are ferocious, and terrifying in the way they possess you and will not let you rest.

Such feelings of anger and hate stem from your awareness that you have been blocked out of someone else's life, in some fundamental way. Before, you had a secure place and a meaning. Now, you have been made invisible, a nonentity, in the life of the one you love, or did once love. You scream to be noticed again, to be valued and respected, and you know that this is not going to happen.

It may be, also, that you have never been properly cared for in the relationship. Perhaps you were never respected or loved, and the relationship was used to control you, limit you, or isolate you. In this case, the anger that surfaces may have been repressed or pushed out of sight for years.

Anger may be difficult, also, if you have been at the receiving end of someone's anger, or even their violence and control, for years. In this case, shame and guilt may be mixed with your own anger: it may be important for you to see that you deserve to be properly cared for and respected, and that your angry energy is there to help you break out and break through to a new place.

This is a key point about anger. It is not just something we should mistrust and repress though it might need that too, in many instances! Instead it can have a positive and forward-looking function. Anger can help to move us on by provoking us to break out of old habit patterns and emotional ruts into a new life. In that process of growth, pain will be involved, but the angry energy will help to lift us over the painful times. Whenever we need to make painful separations from our past, anger is part of the equipment we possess and the dynamism we need.

Forms of Anger

Anger is very difficult for us to accept: it may feel mean-minded, like descending to the level of childish squabbling and trading pointless insults. Yet it is possible to see anger as a vital energy, one of the elements of everyone's personal vitality: an essential part of being human, because it drives our growth and process of maturing. Anger takes many forms, but I will try to separate out three groups of feelings that indicate different channels along which the energy might flow.

The Volcano of Anger

Negative Angry Energy

Anger may be volcanic and volatile, a feeling of uncontrollable force that wells up inside. It may make you shake and seethe inside—an energy you can barely hold within that makes you feel as though your whole inner world might be destroyed by it.

Anger feels fierce, destructive and savage, something primitive and uncivilized. Sometimes it feels violent, unprincipled and untamed: something that might ask anything at all, and not stop until satisfied. It may feel mean-minded and spiteful, using sarcasm and withering insults to get the upper hand.

Anger turns the world chaotic, twisting everything out of shape, distorting words and meanings until truth vanishes, denying the good in everything.

Positive Angry Energy

It may seem strange, but anger can be positive! Anger can speak for you, louder than words. It demonstrates that you need space, and that you are willing to claim your own space and time for yourself. The message is, 'Keep out.' When you have found or made your own space, alone and at a time and place you choose, you can look after the hurt and damaged part of you. You can cry if you wish, scream and shout and wail. But you are insisting that you will do it alone, and that you can come through on your own. Crying is a way of letting the feelings flow out of you: sometimes anger is needed, to create your own privacy to do this safely.

Anger can be highly protective and nurturing. At the end of a relationship, there may be many tangled boundaries that need to be disentangled. There is no time to think, or take skilled advice, or go for counselling. That may follow, later, at an appropriate time. Anger can instinctively protect you, hold you in and enfold you. The message is, 'I can decide alone, for myself: I can look after myself.' In this type of angry energy, you are protecting yourself, vigorously and uncompromisingly.

Anger can be inspiring! You may have devoted years of your life to making the relationship work, to carrying the various burdens of it, negotiating and making allowances. Now is the time for instant action, and anger supplies the energy to leap straight over obstacles, to hit the target and not get side-tracked. Anger can cut through the crap!

Anger can drive your plans. When you need energy to plan your life alone, to see yourself as a separate person, possibly for the first time in your life, and to hold on to your vision, anger may provide the spark that keeps you going.

Anger can 'follow through', and not allow you to stumble at the last hurdle. Sometimes it is easy to pull back, to avoid the final stroke: you can be tempted to hold on to old dreams, to slip back into old expectations, hoping that this might, after all, have been just some horrible dream. At this crucial moment, anger can give you the courage to finish what you started, rather than putting off the inevitable. You are enabled to move on, instead of standing still or sliding back.

Anger can give a visionary edge to what you plan. There is a highly creative side to this energy, which is rarely acknowledged. Anger, in this positive sense, can be prophetic, leading you on beyond the familiar and what you already know. In the situation of separation and divorce, there is nowhere else to go, other than places you probably have never been before—isolation, loneliness, pain—and never wanted to visit! Anger can transform this unexplored territory, giving you leadership for yourself and others in an unknown land.

Directed Angry Energy

In this third category, anger is more like a vigorous, forward-looking and confident striding out. Anger in this sense has no need to hurt anyone else, to win battles or exercise control. All the energy is available to you in a channelled and directed way. There is a heroic quality about it, the sort of lively, indomitable spirit that makes us admire survivors and those who have won through against all the odds. Most 'martial arts' recognize that the main enemies of courage are within oneself, not outside. This is an energy that has become positive from within.

The power of this kind of courageous anger is to forge new paths, to transform obstacles into advantages, to re-invigorate us when we are worn out, to cut through old knots, and to shine in darkened places.

Anger: What to do with the Energy

The problem of anger is how to respect and understand this type of energy, when the feelings are so negative, confused, and despairing, and the whole situation seems out of control, beyond understanding. There is no point in pretending that respecting anger is easy or natural. The anger will well up in you, in its worst possible forms: nothing can stop it, and you may feel terrified, or disgusted at yourself for feeling such things, or even self-destructive.

If you have spent any length of time in a relationship, angry energy may try to follow old patterns—well-defined pathways that have become habitual in the relationship. Anger may flow down these ruts, like water down a channel. It may be very difficult to prevent yourself acting in the old, set patterns—the patterns that were formed in a

The Volcano of Anger

relationship that no longer exists! Such patterns no longer have any meaning, but may be all that you know about how to express your inner needs, simply because you have lived and developed within the relationship for more years than you care to remember!

But now there are immediate and important choices to be made, in a situation that is totally new. You can take charge of what happens to that energy as it surfaces. Will you use anger to attack and destroy your partner, or will you keep your energies for your own inner struggles? Will you use it to undermine him/her in the eyes of the children, or will you maintain everyone's dignity in a very painful situation? Will you use it to disguise your pain and grief under an icy exterior, saving up the poison for later, or will you be honest and angry only as much as you need to be? Will you allow yourself to shrivel up inside and become bitter, or will you hold your damaged self in a place of security, until you have time to heal? Will you splash out your anger in sarcasm and criticism, to try to make someone feel really small, or will you save your energy for the job of rebuilding your life?

Now there are other possibilities, new and different pathways for your energies to follow. The difficulty is in making a start and, even before that, in choosing which path to follow, which action to take. In this completely new situation, it may be difficult to judge what your own motives are, and whether the objectives you have defined are in fact the best ones.

Some choices will lead inevitably to a negative end, or to a hurtful conclusion: they tend to be obvious, and the possibility of hurting your ex-partner may be the tell-tale indicator of a negative trend! Other choices of action are more difficult to predict. Sometimes it is difficult anyway to know what our own motives are when situations are complicated. Sometimes we do the right thing for the wrong reasons! Sometimes what we do for the right reasons seems destined to turn out wrong, repeatedly. We have to live with this sort of uncertainty.

Yet there are times when one pathway, however difficult, seems to lead to a constructive end, or at least to cause the minimum amount of pain to all concerned. This in itself may be an indicator of a positive use of energies, though it will be wise to remember that your ex-partner is no longer 'on the same side' as you, and to take advice from experienced friends!

No one can give any magic answers, because any 'way forward' is unpredictable, and we have to learn as we go along. In addition, any choice you make will be accompanied by the need to grow, and growth in this sense is going to be painful. So any choice is going to be painful!

Accepting and Respecting your Feelings

Anger is a devastating feeling, overwhelming and intense. Yet it is only a part of you, only one feeling among many, even though it feels like everything at the same time. It is vital to 'respect' such feelings. This is a skill, like knowing you are hungry but not eating. We are used to the idea that emotions are overwhelming, and I am not trying to suggest there is some sort of switch which can be flicked off, to stop angry feelings. Feelings are powerful, but we can, if we wish, find a respect for them, and a respectful distance from them.

The point is that we do have an inner sense of ourselves which is always present, no matter how much the waves of emotion sweep over us, and no matter how deep is the ocean of painful feelings. It is the sensation of, 'I am me. I am not only this anger. I am bigger than the anger.' It is the knowledge that this 'me' has always been present, and has sometimes been angry, but often not. This 'me' is the inner sense of someone who is free, who deserves respect and care, who has the potential for growth and change. This inner, free and wholesome spirit has many names in different cultures: in our own, I suspect it has been called the soul or spirit of a person.

One way to 'allow' your own anger but not lose hold of the essential 'me', is to take definite steps to hold yourself, inside, when the anger wells up. You can physically withdraw to a safe place where you can be alone with it: close the door and be alone. Or if the time is not right, make an appointment with yourself, to listen to your anger. You may decide to make notes, or keep a diary or journal. If you are in a stressful meeting, take five minutes out. If you are in no state for a meeting coming up, put it off. All this is evidence that you are treating yourself with respect. You are not denying your anger, but you are saying that this anger is not the whole story, and you will not be driven by it. You can take charge of what you say, when, and to whom, rather than blurting something out while possessed by rage.

Respecting yourself is the key to 'respecting your feelings'. Feelings cannot be switched off, but they can be counterbalanced by other feelings, and you may need to work at respect for yourself: that also is a feeling, because you are placing a value on you! Another key element in all this is to acknowledge that the anger you carry may not be entirely your own! Years of interacting with someone, a partner or parent, who does not recognize his or her own anger, may have left you with a huge load to carry. Sadly, this is especially likely to be true if you are sensitive to other people's emotions. It is precisely people who are sensitive in this way who end up being pulled out of their own true shape by carrying a great weight of emotions from someone else. Finding your own centre, the 'me' inside, will be the start of drawing new lines on your inner map, so that you can recognize what is rightly yours, and what is not yours.

The Volcano of Anger

In all these ways, you can treat your own anger with respect. You can accept that this is a valid part of you. You can listen to the voice of the anger, and hear what the hurt and vulnerable part of you has to say. You can know that this is not all of you, just a part. You cannot cut yourself off from the anger, but equally, you are not at its mercy. It is only a part of you.

This book is not a manual of any sort, and there are many far more explicit and specialized ways to be present with and respect your feelings. You may wish to find out about meditation techniques, or ways of 'centring' or 'focusing' yourself. Counselling or therapy may also be effective for you. A mutual support group, where people who have been through the same experience can share with you and offer their sympathetic understanding, can be wonderful. For men, a group of experienced men might be highly important. The pastoral care of a trusted adviser or priest may also be effective.

What Follows?

One result of this may be that you do not act on your anger immediately. You do not say the first thing that comes to mind, and you do not react when provoked. This can help to break the cycle of defensiveness, which leads so many discussions into arguments and then into rows.

Another result may be that you are freer to listen: anger is felt, but does not come between you and your ability to listen carefully. You can negotiate with a clear head so you may find yourself thinking more slowly and clearly, and insisting that you need time to make a decision instead of being 'hustled' into it. Giving yourself time to find out what you really need and want is important when you are in a painful situation. (It is often so difficult to 'hear' what your needs are.) It may also be true that you are simply unused to paying attention to what you really want: you may have spent years putting your own needs second, within the relationship. In finding time to consider things carefully, you can make sure that what is happening is part of your plan, not part of someone else's; or at least that it does not sabotage your plans completely.

By giving your anger a time and a space, you can also deepen your respect for yourself. You can make room for an aspect of yourself (your angry side) that may have frightened you before, or seemed unworthy, or always seemed to be 'somebody else's fault'. You are opening up an area for new growth: the positive and channelled use of new energies.

In general, the immediate effect of this way of looking at anger is to turn the energy away from short-term strategies. These might include denying the anger, blaming someone else for everything, hating another person, blocking communication, distorting the truth, or just being destructive.

Instead, the energy gets linked to more difficult tasks, the hard work of setting the new boundaries for yourself, and making sure that your point of view is clearly heard. This is the area of facing your own pain, surviving whatever practical challenges you are facing, coping with new routines and important decisions, living in the present not in the past, and generally making a completely new 'you'.

In the longer term, you may choose to look at deeper aspects of your anger, such as how it connects with other features of your life, your childhood, your parents, your job, or whatever. That can all be done when time and opportunity are right. For the moment, you are choosing to allow your anger, but not be dominated by it. You are trying to find ways in which that energy can be used productively and usefully.

In case this seems very easy to say, let me add that anger does not seem to me a simple emotion. Either in its very obvious form (shouting, arguments) or in its more hidden forms (withdrawal, isolation, refusal to co-operate), it is a complex set of feelings, and closely connected with pain. In order to use angry energy productively, pain also has to be faced.

Love and Pain

Separation and divorce tend to bring up profound questions about love and pain. What is love, if it can disappear? How can a committed love 'die'? Can love be the same, before and after a break-up? What has love to do with pain? Why do they seem so inseparable? Breaking up also requires answers to the questions, 'What was it all for? What did it mean?' In this short exploration, I am trying to see the issues that lie beyond the immediate trauma of the divorce or separation, and beyond the practical challenges. The long-term and deeper challenge is concerned with what you really believe in, the roots of why you carry on at all.

Love and pain are an enigmatic couple. To me, love is not the opposite of pain. Love has no opposites! But pain is the opposite of living life fully as far as each of us is able. Each of us has a way of living life that is unique and individual, and pain is evidence that we are in a restricted and unhappy state. Much of the central focus of this book is the problem of that inner pain, and how we can choose to accept the pain, and learn from it, without choosing to dwell on the suffering.

What is 'love'? Is it the misty-eyed romance of youth, the search for the one true love? Is love the full basket of hopes, expectations and idealism with which we generally start our experience of relationships? Is it the romantic ideal expressed through the white wedding, the bells and the lace? Is love rooted in a church wedding and lifelong exclusive commitment? However cynical or worldly-wise we may be, these ideas and meanings are still potent for many people—perhaps most. There is a deep-rooted social and religious expectation of the married couple as the 'building block of society'. Marriage confers social status and respectability, even now. Religious teachings emphasize the family as a reflection of God's own being, or marriage partnership as a reflection of the relationship between Christ and the Church. Implied in all this is an emphasis on eternal commitment and a merging of two souls. Romantic love of the starry-eyed sort is supposed to develop and change, through the 'usual difficulties', into a comfortable companionship and a gentle merging of the two personalities. Difficulties are expected to be surmounted through commitment, gritted teeth, and self-sacrifice 'for the sake of the children'.

If these are the meanings we are all given at the start of the 'marriage journey', by society and religious teachers, we are entitled to ask what 'meanings' are given for other equally common experiences, i.e. that love becomes disillusioned and cynical; that marriage becomes burdensome and disappointing; and that companionship deteriorates into intolerance, disagreements, and outright dislike.

Love and Pain

The truth is that no answer is available. Both Church and Government are beginning to take note of the pressures on marriage and committed relationship, but the response is still at a very early stage. Until now, those breaking up could at best encounter a defeated and resigned sadness; at worst, condemnation and lack of any understanding.

In terms of feelings, first love or first marriage tends to be full of intensity and passion, a sense of adventure and optimism, and a strong feeling of 'rightness'. There is an intention to be committed and respectful towards the beloved. By contrast, breaking up is often full of feelings of sadness, failure, rejection, self-doubt, mistrust, loss of friends and status, guilt, blame and confusion. There may, of course, be feelings of triumph and liberation, but not usually in both partners, and hardly ever without some sadness.

Society fails to deal adequately with the pain of breaking up. We are left to ourselves to work it out. Perhaps that is part of its meaning? By asking about the meaning of pain as well as the meaning of love in breaking up, I am consciously pointing to the individual, subjective and spiritual side of life. This is because I think that is where most of us experience life rather than in our heads, through theories, or through what we have been told to think or believe. I believe we experience life where it makes us cry, either through joy or sorrow, and we know that this is what makes us human. We may, of course, choose to ignore what we experience, or allow its meanings only according to our beliefs, but the experience is still profound and personal.

In 'normal' life, we give a top priority to finding happiness and avoiding pain, and this is almost a 'spiritual' quest; we treat it as a vocation. Nothing is more important than this. Yet, in breaking up, pain is unavoidable. Pain is not a single idea, but has as many meanings for us as happiness. Pain is the dark side of our yearning for perfection. We look for the perfect partner, the perfect children, the perfect home, the perfect job, and the perfect product. Within that yearning for perfection is hidden our ability to ignore our own human imperfections and failings.

To discover the meaning of pain is to embark on a journey of self-discovery. In a way, the whole process of breaking up is a journey of discovery. When starting this journey, we immediately find that meanings cannot be prescribed (by religion, society or community), but are arrived at from within our own experience. We find that relationship (including marriage, break-up and divorce) is not a state but a process. This process, to be alive and true to our humanity, must involve growth, discovery, enlargement, moving beyond old boundaries and ideas about ourselves, and transformation of who we are. Relationships can never be static, and any attempt to hold them at the romantic, starry-eyed phase, is doomed to failure.

Pain and Family Values

In this notion of transformation lies the root of the pain. Pain necessarily accompanies any attempt to grow or change. I believe that, however deep the pain, the process has some meaning, purpose or destination. In applying this view of life to what happens within a marriage or committed relationship, it may be helpful to look at what meanings or values underlie society's often-quoted approval of 'family values'. What is the value system which is so often collectively expressed, and which we take on board from our earliest days? What, in our present culture and society, are the stereotypes of family? I suggest they look something like this:

- material prosperity: a comfortable home
- exclusive sexual fidelity
- long-term commitment
- decisions based on rational understanding
- a heterosexual couple of similar age
- an authoritarian form of education of children using punishments and rewards
- production of 'model' children/consumers
- the search for happiness.

The list has minimal connection with religious wisdom about marriage, or with the experience of previous generations.

Within this rational framework, the usual formulations about how to make marriage work are to do with 'tolerance', 'mutual respect', 'love', 'sticking together', 'acceptance', and all 'for the sake of the children'. Given this framework of values, it is interesting to ask how pain is treated or valued in our collective understanding. I suggest that pain is commonly given the following meanings:

- a treatable illness ('Just take the pills')
- something to conquer ('You can do it!')
- something to reject ('You don't deserve this')
- a problem which just needs a bit of tinkering by the right expert ('Get some therapy')
- someone else's fault ('You were lumbered with that one')
- something to be stoically borne ('Life is no bed of roses')
- a failure to get it right ('Try again somewhere else')
- a just punishment for your mistakes ('You made your bed, now lie in it...')
- a tragedy ('Terribly sad but we can't do anything about it').

I am suggesting that the framework of family or marriage values and the attitudes to pain are no longer valid. People quite rightly have high expectations of life: there is a will to explore our own dignity and inner potential as individuals, instead of accepting an older idea that we are undeserving or sinful. Even though we get it wrong often enough, we also know that life is here for learning, and for an intense voyage of discovery. That is the knowledge that babies and children bring with them into the world, and that is what we so often learn to forget as we grow older.

Pain is a complex phenomenon. On the one hand, we dread it and avoid it at all costs. On the other hand, painful experiences teach us vital lessons in life. In so far as we repress pain, we also repress joy and life. Shutting off suffering and pain also shuts us down into a little, cramped, heavily fortified and defended prison. After a few years of this, we have forgotten what it is like to stretch out and up, and walk freely. Joy disappears, and depression or guilt takes over.

Am I saying that we should like pain? It is more like a feeling that we should give it a proper value, we should respect it. No one gets away without it. Being aware of oneself is a good place to start, and sometimes my awareness tells me that I am in pain, that I hurt, that I am screaming inside. It is important to take that inner pain, to respect it, to look at it steadily, to sit beside it and ask gentle questions. We need to give it time: there is no hurry, because the pain holds the key to a lot of questions that are crucial for us as individuals. And the pain will not go away.

Though pain is a personal challenge, and appears to be 'just' our problem—dealt with behind closed doors, or through gritted teeth, or with a stiff upper lip—it is also a public concern. We know instinctively that pain and death are crucial to life, they give life meaning, in a strange way. What happens to one of us happens to us all. The way each of us deals with pain, with the challenge that pain throws in front of us, is important for all of us.

There are skills in dealing with pain, but they cannot be applied until we accept the reality of pain. Knowing that you are feeling pain is a vital accomplishment. Pretending it does not exist, running away from it, or blaming someone else, is the easiest and most natural thing in the world. But healing cannot start until you know in your bones that the pain belongs to you, and is yours. Others may have a hand in it, but the challenge is yours. Only when you can see the pain is yours can you take up the real power that lies inside you, which can deal with that pain. Only when you do not blame others can you stop blaming yourself.

Men and Divorce

I am writing this section as a man, based on my experience of the loneliness, pain and total isolation that followed my break-up. Due to the prevailing culture, which infects men's upbringing and conditioning with 'macho' stereotypes, I believe that men can encounter specific difficulties with their feelings and self-esteem during divorce and separation. This is what I shall try to address. Once again, the varied experiences of men are introduced by a small sample of five men who responded to my questionnaire.

Men's Stories

How did you learn about the break-up? How long ago? Did you initiate it?

1. My wife announced that she wanted to live on her own (with the children). It happened nine years ago. I did not initiate the break-up.

2. My wife spoke to me and said, 'I no longer wish to be married to you'. It happened ten years ago. I did not initiate the break-up.

3. The process was long and involved. There was no particular point in time, rather a series of points. It happened eight years ago. I initiated it.

4. In our processing together, we both arrived at the same point. It happened four years ago. Neither of us initiated it: it felt much more like a 'joint effort'.

5. I made the decision. It happened over twenty years ago.

What made you most angry?

1. Two things: firstly, my wife did not live on her own, another man moved in; and secondly, I knew we were screwing up the children.

2. The feeling of being cheated, and the selfishness of my wife.

3. That I loved two women and the choice was not easy. The anger was that a choice was expected: the hurt was that I did not want to make the choice.

4. That the promises of a passionate and sexual relationship that had been offered at the beginning had been reneged upon, and that I had given up a marriage to be there.

5. I was very out of touch with my anger at that time.

What made you most hurt?
1.

2. The thought that being 'myself' was not acceptable.

3.

4. That we had been fighting for four years.

5. My inability to work with difficult emotions in myself. My tendency to walk away and not confront them.

What made you most fearful?
1. Fear of the future, fear of being on my own, and fear of losing contact with my children.

2. The fear of loneliness.

3. Losing what I already had (family, home, etc.).

4. Being alone.

5. The unknown. Where I was going. Was it a wise decision?

Did you ever feel very low? If so, when?
1. Yes, for some months after the split.

2. Yes, but not in depression.

3. Yes, before the choice was made. OK once the choice was made.

4. No. I felt much more comfortable with this break-up.

5. On and off. High then low. I thought I was free but I felt trapped by my hunger or desperateness.

What kept you going?
1. Very supportive friends and the love of my children.

Men and Divorce

2. Support of friends, and reading about others in the same situation.

3. It was like wanting to know how it would all end.

4. Wanting to see how the story pans out. (It is more like a film with me as actor, director and script-writer).

5.

What was your best source of help?
1. A good friend advising me to 'take each day as it comes'. This was invaluable.

2. A friend/acquaintance who pointed out that I could see it as a process of change.

3. Friends, therapy, and my faith in 'the story'.

4. I had few friends at this time and wasn't in therapy, but my trust in the process was very strong.

5. I do not think I had any concept of help. I just reached out towards other women in a very haphazard way.

What do you regret most?
1. Not being able to discuss the implications sufficiently at the time with my wife.

2. The *death* of trust.

3. That my wife and I did not go for couple counselling before I made the choice.

4. The fighting: what a waste of time!

5. The brutal way I ended it but then exploited my ex-lover's need.

Are you in a better place now?
1. Yes.

2. Yes. I have dealt with my fear of loneliness.

3. Yes.

4. Yes. Quite unexpectedly, my wife asked me to return.

5. Yes—hard to compare to how I was then.

What did the experience give you?
1. A realization that nothing can be taken for granted. Humans need continuously to explore and experience the phenomenal complexities of relationships.

2. All part of life's rich pattern, and learning by experience.

3. There was a great confusion in me about being comfortable and needing to be passionate.

4. I am still not sure where my passion can be put but I now feel softer, stronger and more tolerant of myself and my wife.

5. The realization that I could be on my own and survive. I found I was more self-reliant than I had expected.

The Social and Cultural Background

In my experience, men are not generally 'in touch' with the subtleties of their own emotional state in intimate relationships. I will generalize a little and speak as a man out of my own experience, but I believe this point of view to have some relevance to men generally. We (men) are not confident in relationships, and have acquired, through childhood experience and conditioning, the ability to ignore our feelings at will. Emotional disturbance within an intimate relationship may be ignored, or treated as 'just how things are', until drastic measures become inevitable. By this time, it may be too late to save the relationship.

Whereas women may be more vividly aware of the ebb and flow of the relationship, men are much more likely to be locked into 'unfeeling' states, by their upbringing and the expectations of those around them. The accepted self-images are of 'the hard man', the worker, the one who is in control of the situation, the one who knows what needs to be known about the practical problems. To be anything else, as a man, seems impossible, unthinkable, or shameful.

Men and women differ, but not in the way that the traditional gender stereotypes would have us believe. I believe that men are every bit as 'sensitive' as women: women are as sensitive as men! Both sexes start off very much the same, but the conditioning imposed on men from their earliest infancy makes it extraordinarily difficult for them to acknowledge their own needs, their loving and warm personalities. Scientific studies show that girl babies are far more likely to get cuddles and caresses than boy babies. Boys are seen as needing to be tough, right from the start—even when they are still in their cradles! It is not surprising that men tend to get locked into an armour-plated self-awareness.

Studies also show that boys are disciplined more than girls, treated more harshly, and laughed at if they cry. Playgrounds are a battlefield of rough justice, survival of the toughest, and macho poses. Boys become experts in bullying and gang warfare, experts in terror, in both inflicting it and feeling it. Competition tends to be encouraged and taken to extremes, becoming the keynote of every encounter, whether sport, exam results, practical skills, dress, girlfriends, or gangs. The prevailing culture is one of all-out competition, winner-take-all battles, and bitterly contested pecking orders enforced by punitive codes. In the office, on the commuter train or on the motorway, on building sites or on the beach, men compete until they drop.

As a result, boys and men can become adept at ignoring their emotional and receptive personalities. They habitually repress their warm and loving natures. They deny their needs for being held, treasured, nurtured and encouraged. Life seems hard, and they adopt a critical, aloof style, with an emphasis on what is intellectual, practical, and hard-nosed, or unemotional. Detachment and objectivity become key words—being 'cool'. What is important is being good at what you do, effortlessly, and not caring how you reach the top, so long as you get there. Life becomes cold and difficult, and success the only measure of being alive: that is, being able to get what you want, when you want it, and to take whatever you need. Men become locked into patterns of satisfying their deeper needs through narrow, specific channels, e.g. careers, money, beer, sex, football. It is important to avoid discussing anything emotional or 'heavy'. Friendship with other men is frowned upon, with the unspoken threat that you will be branded as 'homosexual'. Personal pain or struggle is treated with laughter, with embarrassment, or with alcohol.

When Men are in Pain

Starting from such a point of not knowing what their own inner feelings truly are, I suspect that men may have a long journey ahead, to define their real differences from women, and the real, unique contributions they can make to marriage, relationship, and parenting. In the present climate, it is much easier for men to look at the powerful and assertive images of women, and not know their own special strengths.

However, when a man encounters the emotional shock and trauma of separation or divorce, all the conditioned denials of his feelings act as a powerful disadvantage, before, during and after divorce. This does not mean that women are more able to find divorce an easy or pleasant experience. It suggests to me that there is more to the story than just the stereotype of the feckless father and the deserted mother and children.

Most divorces are initiated by women, so men are being forced to face these issues more and more. It seems that the younger a man is at divorce, the less likely he is to be able to rebuild his life and achieve his ambitions. Young men are vulnerable, despite their tough exteriors. Men are suffering, and are not able to face their own pain, because of the built-in, habitual denials that they are feeling pain. Other men do not help, because they also are denying pain, and also are looking for someone to blame. The prevalence of suicide, as the biggest cause of death in all men between twelve and sixty, bigger even than death on the roads, indicates how much men are paying the penalty for their prematurely closed feeling natures and loving personalities.

On top of this, a legal system that perpetuates social myths, e.g. that men make inadequate or inferior parents, puts men into a defensive position in any disputes around property or contact with children. Men are likely to perceive their final situations as the result of having been victimized and exploited.

On the other side of the coin, I will re-state in the strongest possible terms that some men are abusive. Most victims of domestic violence or sexual abuse are women, and there is no excuse for violence against a partner or spouse or child—be it physical violence, threats of violence, intimidation, sexual abuse, deprivation, personal ridicule, isolation, mind games, or controlling behaviours of any kind.

Equally, there can be no excuse for men who continue to abuse or victimize women during a separation, or use divorce/legal proceedings as a weapon to inflict hurt and pain. No matter who left whom, if men are to gain some primary freedoms as fathers—if they are to be recognized in their own right as nurturers, carers and members of the 'essential team'—then women also have much to gain through being acknowledged as independent and freedom-loving individuals, not stereotyped as mothers and partners.

What is the Baseline for Men?

The full range of men's capacities can easily be overlooked. It may be that it does not need saying, but men can be:
- loving
- loyal and faithful

- determined and principled
- playful and good fun
- dynamic and inspiring
- creative and inspired
- soft and sensitive
- passionate and sexually free
- strong and far-sighted
- caring and illuminating.

Women can be all these things too! But it seems easier to forget the full range of men's capabilities, or to believe that men are simply incapable of these things.

Men need other men, and they need guidance from older men. Young boys in school need male teachers, while adolescent boys need male mentors and role models. For a fuller treatment of men's needs, see the booklist at the end of this book.

Men and Sex

In the scenario of breaking up, of being left, a man may feel that he is losing everything he has possessed or shared or worked for, and everything he has desired, or is permitted to desire. He is caught in a Catch-22 of loving someone no longer available to him, and feeling unable to love in any other way. Deep emotional dependency on the relationship can result in hatred of women and a desire to exploit women for sex, in revenge—but using desire in this way can only lead a man away from his centre. It will not help him to grow.

In an environment where men's feelings are so denied, seen in a distorted way, or narrowed, it is not surprising that sex comes to play an extraordinary part in men's lives. I tend to see sex more in the full rainbow of its emotional meanings, and less as a reproductive mechanism or 'drive'. Hence, sex may be:
- a beacon: a guiding light
- something entirely autonomous and unquestioned, beyond question
- a precious way of breaking out of the hardened 'shell' of the body
- a touchstone or compass within a relationship
- the only warm feeling in a sea of cold, hard reality
- a way of escaping loneliness
- a solitary point of emotional contact
- the main indicator of 'love' in relationship, and its main proof
- the first and principal route to loving feelings.

Equally, in a reverse light, it is the point of a man's greatest vulnerability:

- where a man loses self-control, or feels controlled (the myth that men are helpless when gripped by sexual desire).

- the place of the 'siren', who can lure a man to destruction.

- the place of shame and shameful feelings, of hesitation, confusion and embarrassment.

- an activity tainted with centuries of religious condemnation and prejudice.

- the point in a relationship which can be most easily contaminated with frustration, anger and accusation.

Rediscovering your Centre

Following on from the sense of being totally destabilized by a break-up, how does a man find himself, his centre ground? And how does he hold himself in his centre? Again, much of this applies just as much to women as men, but I believe that men tend to need their neediness emphasized, because they are much less skilled in identifying their inner needs: knowledge of this tends to be blocked at source, for the reasons I have already specified. The following are positive measures that could help.

- Reclaim the past: re-visit and know again the special places of your past, however much it hurts. The shared past needs to be disentangled, so that you can keep what is yours, rather than trying to throw everything out and forget.

- Accept the present and treasure every moment, especially with your children.

- Respect your ex-partner—if you can. If not, respect their separateness.

- Make a book of special photographs: it celebrates the past and keeps it safe, so you can move on.

- Similarly, pack up the past: collect letters, mementoes and other items into a box, and seal it up. Store it safely for your children. Look to the future with a clear heart.

- Find a way to establish your own wholeness, especially if you are feeling fragmented and shattered: get in touch with deep things, walk on the mountains, find wild places, be alone.

- Be unafraid of your pain: invoke eternal values and find a perspective on your own pain, a context for your suffering; if you are religious, the Church will provide this. If not, look to myth and the old stories.

- Help others: join clubs, be active in the community and find your worth.

- Talk to men who have shared similar experiences. Find therapy or therapeutic courses.

- Find your unique talents and activate them again—perhaps things that you gave up because you married or were too busy.

- Create a home for yourself that expresses the unique 'you': decorate, cook, be sociable, make it comfortable, original and exciting.

- Renew who you were before your partnership, and discover that you are still changing and growing.

Accept and celebrate your sexual yearning! Far from being a source of pain, shame or torment, your sexuality is multi-faceted and extraordinary. Celebrate:
- your vigour and strength
- your yearning for closeness
- your capacity for loving intimacy
- your naked, raw energy
- your protective and nurturing power
- your damaged emotions around sex, with all the guilt and shame
- your ability to re-make and re-find your desire.

Be, feel, and think positively!
- Communicate: do not hold it all in! Practise self-awareness.
- Challenge yourself: commit yourself to transformation.
- Cradle your sadness, and know that it is not all of you, only part.
- Channel your energies. Find a way to use the energy of your anger:
    a) through physical activity: sport, martial arts or yoga, home-making and DIY, walking, cycling, climbing, swimming;
    b) through learning new knowledge about yourself: find and read books; get therapy; find inspiring people or teachers; join groups for mutual support;
    c) devise plans and strategies: make a life plan, put your dreams and visions onto paper, get them ready; learn mediation and negotiation skills; learn time management skills—necessary for balancing your life and the time you give to your children; be aware of your ideals and abilities, and your needs.

Children: Responsibility and Agony

I have just two stories to introduce what is a brief survey of children's needs when their parents split up, and their special perspective on what happens. Similar questions to those used on the questionnaire were answered.

The Boy's Story

How did you learn about the break-up?
The long protracted high-volume arguments; the silences and tensions. Mother's long periods crying, and father's raised voice. Younger brother seemed more aware of what was happening than I was. Father told us we were moving with him to a town nearby. Some months later, mother told us she did not want us to go: in tears, crying and cuddling us for some forty-five minutes. I was aged eleven.

What made you most angry?
I was not angry at the time, not consciously until I was nineteen.

What made you most hurt?
Not hurt: upset. Missing my mother. My father's temper.

What made you most fearful?
I am not aware, have never been aware, of fear.

Did you ever feel very low?
I felt very low seven years later when my first girlfriend left me. I was only then acutely aware of the loss of my mother.

What kept you going?
Inherited bloody-mindedness, and a certain amount of self-abuse through pain control in exercise through sport.

What was your best source of help?
Mental internalization, especially while running. A kind of meditation and inner calm.

What do you regret most?
Regret? What's the point?

Children: Responsibility and Agony

Are you in a better place now?
Yes. Why? Essay question!

What did the experience give you?
In essence, I've learned about pain and loss, and the viability of some coping strategies. This affects insights in relationships with others and aids discussions about helping myself and others cope with pain and loss.

The Girl's Story

It started off as a normal life, with me, my sister and my Mum and Dad. And then, one day when we came back from our Nan's on the train, Mum said, 'Your Dad's going to take you home in the car, but then he's going to go away.' And I was so shocked, it came to me so suddenly. I was really frightened about where was Dad going, and I wished they had really talked to me about it.

Looking back to when my Mum and Dad were still together, I think that it would not have worked out even if they did carry on living together. They were always arguing and things, and when they had split up—quite a while after—I remember sitting on the stairs and hearing Mum crying, and talking to my Dad and arguing with him. Then I did not know what to think, and now I am still wondering why they were arguing all the time, because I used to think they went together.

At the actual Registry Office, as Mum and my step-dad were saying the words for the marriage, I felt as if all the family were becoming really close. At the same time I was thinking that me and my sister were getting further apart from my Dad. I think my step-dad's boys must be kind of feeling a bit like that too, about their Mum, and that was one thing that I was not really very happy about. But I am still OK about it now.

I think, on the whole, my life's been a good one. I have been doing loads of things, and I have achieved lots of things. I'm good at art and music, and I've got loads of friends at school, but what's really annoying is I often get jealous of my friends. I always think they have got a nice life still, just Mum and Dad, I mean my new family is still just as nice but it is just a bit different. I am still wondering what my life would have been like if it was still just my Mum and my Dad, and me and my sister.

Worries and Fears

In this section I use the term 'parents' to include foster-parents, adoptive parents, step-parents, and anyone who is in the position of main care-giver. The emotions and responsibilities are very similar, even to the depth and strength of feeling about the child. The feeling of responsibility for children is a knife in the heart of most parents—fear for their safety and well-being is the one great dread of a parent's life. But along with the vulnerability of babies and children comes the precious gift that they bring into your life, and the amazing realization of the life that you have passed on, or are nurturing in them, and which flowers day by day. So nothing hurts more than the dread that you will be held responsible for destroying their childhood, ruining their chances in life, and letting them down when they needed you.

In contrast to the worries usually expressed, I offer a set of arguments that may help to counter-balance the extreme emotions that can arise, in this aspect of divorce as in any other.

'What about the children: what will happen to them?'
'What about the damage to the kids?'
'I am/we are ruining their lives.'
Children have life in them, of their own: they need our protection and our love, but not our fears and anxieties. Worrying about them is only healthy when we are concerned about them as individuals, not when we are seeing them as an extension of us or a walking proof that we are 'good' parents.

'We mustn't hurt the kids.'
'Anything is better than breaking up.'
'They need their Mum and their Dad.'
Children do need their mum and dad, but not locked together in an unloving, unforgiving marriage. Children are as much damaged by hatred in a marriage, as by bitterness at its ending.

'I feel like a criminal, leaving them.'
'What will people think of me?'
'No one will ever understand.'
The answer to 'What will people think of me?' is 'What do I really think of myself?' Only I can understand what I do, and only I can accept myself. The acceptance (or rejection) of anyone else is relatively much less important. What children need to know is that, even though their mum and dad choose to end the marriage, they will never choose to end being parents. Children need to know that a parent's decision is NOT THEIR FAULT. They need to understand that the parent is an adult, and has made an adult choice which is not the fault or responsibility of the child. The parent is going to stop being a husband or wife or partner, but will never stop being the child's mum or dad.

The child needs this reassurance, even though no guarantees can be given about life,

Children: Responsibility and Agony

and even though some parents are more skilled than others. If the parent is not a danger to the child, his or her dependable and regular input to the child's life continues to be vital.

'I'll be there for them when they really need me.'
'I'll see them regularly and keep tabs on them.'
'I'll be in a better place for the kids when I'm away from him/her.'
It is perfectly possible to love children at a distance, though this is not our natural instinct, and it is more difficult to carry out within the structures of our society, which is geared up for the 'nuclear family' structure (as much as it is supportive of any family structure). Many separated parents share responsibilities, offer different but complementary caring, and maintain separate homes for their children. The question is, do you really believe you can do it? Children will be crucially concerned to know whether you are sure about this, or are prepared to do your best. If you are, their anxiety will be greatly reduced.

'They're tough, they'll make it OK.'
'They don't need me.'
'He/she has always been better than me with the kids.'
Children will always need their parents. Their life energy will carry them a long way without you, but somewhere in them will be a void, which only you can fill. No matter how awkward you felt with them, and how much you felt like a useless parent, they still need you. Divorce or separation is precisely the time to recognize your unique role in their lives, whether as father or mother.

'I hate the little brats.'
'He's/she's spoiled them rotten.'
'It's too late for me to do them any good.'
Children are separate human beings, full of their own character and energy, even from the moment of birth (and probably before!). They are not involved in what you feel about your partner, and they want nothing more than to love both of you, and be completely fair to you both. It is never too late for you to add your special contribution to their lives.

'He/she doesn't deserve the kids.'
'I'll take them away.'
'I'll make sure they know what he/she has done.'
Children have a right to both parents. No one, not even the other parent, has the right to remove them from a parent unless they are in some kind of danger. Putting pressure on children in order to distort their loving feelings, or to prejudice them against the other parent, will in the end rebound against you. One day they will grow

up, and recognize that you have used them, by not telling the truth, or twisting it, or leaning on them when they were too young. I know that the grief of the ending of a relationship can make it extremely difficult to see children's needs (your own needs may be overwhelming) but it is precisely at this time that their needs are most acute. Any kind of balance that you can keep, in your feelings about your ex-partner, will be vital for your children's peace of mind.

How do Children React?

Often, children cannot believe what you are saying, when you announce that you are splitting up. The news is best conveyed by both of you, at a quiet time and in a matter-of-fact way that reassures, without seeking to hide the pain. Younger children may imagine that nothing will really change, and will continue to believe this until someone actually packs bags and walks out of the door. Very small children, even babies, will know that something is different, especially if their routine is affected. Young children will continue to ask, 'When is Daddy/Mummy coming home?' Older ones will show sudden and unexpected changes in behaviour, such as getting into trouble at school or going into moods.

Children will tend to blame you for what has happened, whether or not you were at fault. They will seem to lose trust in life, or in you. If you are the main care-taking parent, they will resent having only you. Try not to take these emotions at face value: taking them personally is a recipe for alienating the children even further. Such judgements will dwindle, and the children will come to a better understanding of you as time goes on. Give them space to grieve, to react, to show their pain. You will need that space yourself. Above all, remember that children need to know that you can take whatever they dish out, without yourself becoming upset. They need you to be strong, and to see clearly where they are themselves lost and blind. Be their strength not their judge: find it in yourself.

Later on, after the actual break-up, children may have high hopes of the 'absent' parent: no matter how much it pains you, their joy at the thought of going to visit, or at how much money they will have spent on them, will be irrepressible. Even if they never see the other parent, they will have idealized images of him/her, and some part of a child may always pine for the person they never really knew or had a chance to be with. Children visiting the other parent will go into unpredictable moods just before they go, and for about two hours after they return. Don't be surprised. They are working themselves up to crossing a giant mountain range into another land, the territory of your ex-partner; and then they have to do it all backwards when they return.

Children: Responsibility and Agony

Children will often seek to protect both parents equally, if they can. Obviously, if one parent has been violent, or abusive, or neglectful, a child can and will make a judgement about that behaviour. But a child will try unremittingly to be fair to each parent, and to protect both if they appear to be suffering. They will attempt to do this without hurting anyone else. A child's sense of fairness is often astonishingly sensitive. Children can also pick up your feelings, so it is important not to lean on them. You cannot hide your anger or pain, but beware of dumping your emotions on children, or allowing them to pick up exaggerated attitudes from you when you are exhausted or suffering. The best antidote to any tendency to lean on your children for support and comfort is to find your own support through friends and trusted advisers.

A child will often seek to please both parents. As you will instantly recognize, trying to please two different people, who may have extremely antagonistic feelings about each other, puts the child into a no-man's land of conflicting emotions. Do your best to help him or her to get through without getting blown up. Understand that their hearts are tender and that every comment you make may be taken to heart, and every time you misunderstand their attempts to bring peace, you may be hurting their very core. The best you can give, in a situation in which there can be no clear-cut answers, is your steadiness of heart, and a clear faith in what you are doing, based on faith in yourself and not blaming anyone else. Faith in yourself, by the way, does not mean you cannot make mistakes. You may, but you also have the determination to press on and set things straight afterwards.

Children will often show changes in mood, becoming resigned and depressed, or else agitated and hyper-active. They may be spiteful to friends or brothers and sisters, irritable or argumentative; or they may lose all interest in school and friends, and show embarrassment about you and their home. At the other extreme, some children become excessively diligent in school, losing themselves in schoolwork and getting high marks. This also may be a reaction, and it may end suddenly during some future crisis not connected to the break-up. Most worrying, children may produce violent 'scenes' or emotional outbursts, for which you are totally unprepared because they have never behaved in this way before. Once again, they need your patience and strength of character. Allow them space to react against what must seem to them a cruel and hard fate. Losing a parent at home is a body blow, and nothing you can do will deflect that blow. However, love is what they are crying out for, and love is what both parents must give.

What Questions do Children Ask?

This section contains questions which children have put to me, and some suggested answers. These are not the only questions, and only general suggestions are given. Other answers may be more appropriate to your situation, e.g. to the age and understanding of the child. The books listed will provide more insights and help.

What is divorce?
Divorce is hard for everyone but it is hardly ever the 'fault' of one person. It is the legal end of a marriage. Partners do not live together any more. They lead separate lives, and you can be part of both because your parents never stop being your mum and dad. Divorce means big changes in your family life; it need not mean the end of it.

Why do we need to talk about divorce?
Talking can help you to understand and can make you feel better. It helps us learn more about ourselves by asking questions and exploring fears. Talking lets other people know how we feel and lets us know how they feel so we see that we are not alone and can try to help each other. It can help us to make sense out of confusion. Sometimes talking helps us to build bridges so that our families can change and develop.

Why does it happen?
It is very difficult to know why. People often marry when they are in love, but actually living with someone else can be very difficult. Marriage may not live up to the expectations of the two people: they feel they need more, or something different. People find they want different things, are not compatible, feel stuck. Respect for the other person may wear thin or vanish and sometimes love turns into hate, or dullness, or boredom. When partners grow up and change they find that they do not suit each other any more: they just do not go together.

What happens to the children in a divorce?
Children often live with their mother, but they can also live part of the time with their dad—sometimes it is shared, half and half! One in ten single parents are dads. Parents may divorce each other, but they can never 'divorce' their children. Some parents do lose touch with their children: often the dad finds it too difficult or painful to be regularly in touch.

Why aren't children told?
Parents may believe the children will be less hurt the less they know, or that they do not need to know much. Sometimes they think children know already or that they

Children: Responsibility and Agony

know more than they do. Parents do not realize that children are more hurt by not knowing.

Is it my fault?

It is not your fault if parents do not want to live together. There is nothing you can do to make them stay together if they want to be apart. It is not your responsibility to keep grown-ups happy! All families have quarrels, and all children do things that parents say are 'naughty'. It is natural and normal to have disagreements with parents and to behave in ways they do not want, but nothing you may have done could have caused the divorce.

How can you tell what is happening?

You can't always tell: some people argue a lot but always kiss and make up. If it is serious, the quarrels are usually about deeper differences, not the everyday things people disagree about.

How do children feel?

There are a whole range of feelings and sometimes lots of different feelings at the same time. It can be hard to know what you are feeling but here are some:
- powerless
- guilty about being unable to cope
- sad and frightened
- guilty and responsible for the break-up
- no one is listening to me
- it's not fair
- they've ruined my life
- ignored by parents: invisible
- thrown about by parents' emotions
- protective about parents, or brothers and sisters
- forced to listen to complaints and bad-mouthing and unfairness
- really upset and angry; scared
- lost and alone in a strange world
- withdrawn, unable to talk, depressed
- confused and shocked: 'my whole world is shattered'
- numb and disbelieving; guilty about not feeling much
- mixed up, a bundle of mixed emotions
- like 'piggy in the middle'
- like a bargaining counter
- like a messenger carrying messages
- sad and strange to leave home to visit one parent, to write to someone who always used to be there, or leave behind someone so important

- fearful and withdrawn
- angry and easily upset
- in a bad mood
- worried all the time
- relieved!

What does it do to children?
Children react differently. Some feel 'odd one out', 'weird', ashamed, or out of sorts while others are angry because they feel that their parents have failed them but, in the end, they often find that they are better off with one parent at a time, instead of two who fight. For a while, some children feel that they are looking after a parent rather than the other way round. Many children feel insecure and fear losing friends and other important people in their lives. Sometimes it is hard to concentrate at school.

What's it like, living in two homes?
It is like living in two different worlds with different ideas about what is important, with different rules about bedtimes, mealtimes and chores. Life can feel busy with weekend visits and travelling. Sometimes it means that you cannot see your friends when you want to because you are on a visit and you have to find new ways of keeping in contact with friends and your absent parent—letters, phone and e-mail. On anniversaries, birthdays and feast days like Christmas you sometimes feel sad and split, wanting to be in both homes at the same time.

How does it feel for the adults?
Like losing a best friend: once you shared all your secrets, but now your best friend just annoys you. The adults have lots of feelings—angry, downhearted, guilty, shocked, betrayed, paralysed, sad, desperate and sometimes vengeful. Sometimes they feel lots of these things at the same time.

What breaks up relationships?
Usually several factors will contribute to the break-up of a relationship. Among them are: lack of trust; money worries; arguments; unemployment or losing a job; overworking or both parents working; constantly moving house; not having supportive friends and family nearby; bad housing; long-term illness or dependency; unfaithfulness; loss of attraction; violence or abuse; simply losing the sparkle between you. A couple may split up for some of these reasons or for other reasons known to them.

What happens afterwards?
Parents do not get over divorce quickly. Usually they have to cope with less money, and single parents have more to do, so they can get tired and worn out. Parents can become good friends, in the end, though some leave home and cannot bear to come back. Some might feel that they would make their children too unhappy if they continued to see you and they cannot cope with the complications.

How do the grown-ups cope afterwards?
Adults may need lots of support from family and friends after a break-up. Most adults need lovers and partners. There may be new brothers and sisters to get to know, if one or both parents start a new family.

What do children need?
With questions like those listed above in their minds, sometimes unspoken, *children need people who will listen*, not only to their words but to their non-verbal communication, people *who will provide them with a secure place that does not change, and lots of time and understanding.* Parents who are breaking up their relationship are not always in the best place to supply all these needs because they have emotional needs of their own to handle. There may be others who want to help. Sometimes the best support that can be given to both parents and children is to be a friend to the children. Here grandparents can have a special role; so can other adults in the family who can provide that sense of security and continuity that is vital for children. Between them, parents and others, including grandparents and the children's friends, might ensure that children's needs are met.

In addition to the above, children need:
- to know they are not alone and others have been through similar experiences
- to know that lots of other children share the same thing
- encouragement to say what they really feel and really need
- plenty of space to be themselves
- lots of trust and the power to make choices
- to learn how to say what they feel when one parent complains about the other
- time to talk with parents and siblings, time to ask questions
- to know that parents can cope, no matter how sad they seem
- to know that parents can find other sources of help
- not to be pressured to take sides with parents
- to know that children sometimes need help and have the right to ask for it
- to know that someone is usually willing to listen
- reassurance about seeing each parent in a different home: it will be OK!
- to know that parents' love for each other is different from their love for you

- to know that parents can love you in different ways, depending on whether they are feeling tired, happy, sad, angry, etc.
- to know that your feelings will change, and get better!
- to know that it is OK to be upset, to grieve, to cry, to be really angry, to protest, to feel the injustice, to shout and argue, to take time for themselves, to stay in, not go to clubs, not do homework
- to learn coping strategies for anger, e.g. exercise, talk, walking away
- help to know that things really do get easier, and they really do get better.

Healing, Restoration, and the Discipline of Love

Language and Perspective

To encounter divorce in your personal life is to encounter a deep shock, a challenge to all your beliefs and values, whether religious or not. Many questions need to be asked and answered. The language we use, and the frame of reference we rely upon, can help or hinder us in answering such questions. These theological reflections outline a framework or context in which profound questions can usefully be explored: it is one that is not currently available to many people.

It is easy, but wrong, to accept the current 'scientific' or descriptive language, which looks at marriage exclusively in terms of 'couples' and 'relationships'. In fact, the meeting of two unique individuals in a loving commitment, their joining together, and their continuing life together, is a series of events wholly mysterious and full of different meanings. Religious language and theological reflection can allow for the expression of some meanings, and indeed truths, which would otherwise remain hidden. Sadly, for many people, the rejection of anything religious because it is automatically classed as 'blinkered' or 'judgemental' can leave painful questions only partially answered. Issues remain unexplored because one possible source of illumination is being ruled out.

Ideas on Marriage

In the Christian tradition, marriage was once seen as an instrument for 'the avoidance of fornication'. We can now take a less mechanistic and judgemental view of sexuality. We can applaud the settled, companionable and committed relationship of two people as the most flexible and durable way to bring up children.

In addition, a modern view of marriage will emphasize its ability to heal and restore each partner, and this is shown in the deep acceptance of one by the other: one imperfect human being accepts, in love, the imperfections of another. In this way, pain and hurt experienced previously may receive some measure of help and healing. Seeing marriage as a 'sacrament' means that it can be seen as 'an outward and visible sign of an inward and spiritual grace'. Healing acceptance, ministered through marriage, becomes a means of divine action in the world. It also becomes a symbol of divine restoration, an example of the divine will for the perfection of creation. The healing is one element of a greater plan, one step in the divine dance. This places marriage in a context of meanings quite different from contemporary frameworks, which may make the search for happiness, sexual or otherwise, the most important perspective.

What about Divorce?

What happens when the Church is challenged to explain the present-day frequency of divorce and partnership breakdown? One possible reaction, also echoed outside the Church, is simply to state the obvious legal position—marriage is based on a promise, and promises should be kept despite all the difficulties. Such a position insists that a promise is only a promise when it is hard to keep; until then, it is merely a statement of intention. But this leaves out the human side of marriage, in favour of imposing a contractual interpretation. Yet marriage was made for humanity, not the other way around! Furthermore, a legalistic way of looking at marriage will also produce the loss of its healing function, precisely when all the hurt in the partnership is crying out for healing.

Another possible response is to say that separation is possible but not divorce. This appears to accord with Jesus' words in the gospel. However, this response is to mistake what is said in controversy for an attempt to state the law. When the scribes ask, 'What can I get away with?' Jesus responds with, 'This is what you are called to.' Such a reaction to divorce also begs the question of what is meant by marriage: what does it mean, if it does not involve living together, sharing bed and board?

A third possible response involves the meaning of adultery. Nowadays, we should probably say that adultery is emotionally significant but, even up to recent times, concern about adultery has had more to do with property and inheritance than the emotional well-being of either partner! That someone other than the husband's child might inherit the husband's property was thought sufficient for divorce—and also sufficient to explain why, though a man might divorce his wife for adultery, a wife had no right to divorce a husband for this.

Perhaps we need a new interpretation of adultery for today's world, one that deals with what might cause adultery in either partner? The essence of this new interpretation might well be illuminated by Milton's wise advice to frame laws that human beings have some chance of keeping. Milton warns us not to set our sights on standards of behaviour that would put inhuman demands upon us, especially in this most delicate and subtle area of human life.

The Discipline of Love

To move to what might seem a more liberal view, though it is one that in reality demands a discipline of a deeper kind, we have to remember that we are created by and for love. Realizing this means that I do not ask, 'Do I love my partner?' but instead must discover what is the demand of love on me—which is a different matter. This attitude will acknowledge my subordination to God. Following from this is the realization that, as only the people involved can decide on the commitment of marriage, so only they can decide whether to divorce.

Christian discipleship is about learning to let love play on us and through us—and this will be painful at times, and at other times joyful. Marriage is no different. The marriage relationship is meant to be a framework and a school for love, but there is a danger of making the institution of marriage an idol. It is impossible to say that staying in a marriage is the one overriding priority. There are those who have stayed in abusive relationships and been embittered, and those who have stayed in similar relationships and shown fruits of love in their lives. Both for those who stay together and for those who divorce, might we not seek to enable them to change from looking at *breaking up* to seeing themselves as *breaking through*?

There will be pain, whatever decision is taken, but such questions as 'What is being sacrificed to what and for what purpose?' need to be asked. Marriage is to be a framework on which a flower may grow. Without marriage, it may be that it cannot grow at all. But marriage in itself is not the flower, and in this it follows the pattern of all discipline in the Christian life. 'Discipline', in its original sense, is about a journey of learning, not about punishment. Asking difficult questions, and making difficult choices, is part of this discipline of love.

Looking Back: Self-examination

As we move from thinking about divorce to thinking about the time after the breaking up of a relationship, there is a place for looking back, for self-examination. In any process of self-examination—and especially when the person involved is already likely to be depressed—there is a great need to beware of defensiveness. Defensiveness can take many different forms. It can include re-writing the past, mockery, shifting blame, and despondent resignation, rather than a positive and accepting resignation. There is also false guilt, which can get in the way of true self-knowledge and can be another form of defence. For instance, I 'own up' to a seemingly acceptable fault, such as working long hours, and use this to hide some other fault, such as refusal to engage with my partner. Effectively, I have put recognition at work above the needs of my marriage.

Self-examination, to be productive in the long term, needs time. Months or years may need to pass, as we slowly absorb the pain and see the lessons of what we have been through. Self-examination must also be conducted, in any Christian setting at least, on the fundamental recognition that God has made us each for himself, that our pain is his, and that the process of self-examination is part of the work of restoration. It is the restoration of hope, the calm acceptance of God's will, and the ability to follow our path in faith, which are the goals of self-examination.

If issues appear, during self-examination, which seem to have nothing to do with the specific relationship, it may well be that they are more appropriately dealt with outside the setting of penitential practice, for instance within a setting of counselling or mutual support. The support of the Church extends to knowing when other professional helpers may be of particular use.

The task of the Church may be formulated in different ways—as the reconciliation of the penitent, the healing of the hurt, the proclamation of God's kingdom, or the extension of the worship of God—but any action by the Church that excludes someone or brands them a leper just because they have been through a divorce, is a serious dereliction.

Institutional Examination

At this point it is worthwhile to consider the place of a wider (and usually neglected) form of self-examination: institutional self-examination. We often seem to reduce sin or failure exclusively to the level of the individual. However, why should two people whose marriage has broken up be made to bear sole responsibility for the assumptions, pressures and temptations handed out by society or the Church?

The fact that there are increasing numbers of marital breakdowns does not indicate that so many more people have suddenly become more selfish or weaker than people of earlier generations. Such figures may indicate that people might have sought divorce had it been available then. Equally, the figures may indicate that the pressures on marriage have changed, and that the reason for the high divorce rate does not lie solely with individuals. There are difficult questions to be asked.

For instance, are there things in society that the Church needs to challenge in order to protect marriage? Has the Church itself made demands or put pressures on couples that have contributed to the breakdown of marriage? Has the Church taken on too readily the assumptions of the surrounding culture—including the assumed right to happiness, and the cult of 'success' in marriage and parenthood as well as in material things?

Every marriage needs support from its beginning, and there is a positive and wide-ranging ministry of marriage support that the Church has only recently begun to recognize. Just as preparation for old age must begin in youth, so preparation for marriage must begin from childhood. There is no point saying to married couples that marriage is one of the building blocks of society if society is not ready to foster and protect marriage.

In this sort of searching enquiry, what are the issues we cannot afford to ignore? The intense interest in sex, of course, but equally the provision of paternity leave. Matters such as working time, the provision of leisure, the idolatry of wealth, and the development of friendships must be pursued. There will be a challenge to the contract-based model of behaviour by which so many are prepared to live. Contracts are all very well, but part of the meaning of marriage is that there is no 'appeal', legal or otherwise, against the decision of a partner. Finally, we can recognize that problems in the relationships of one generation can only be addressed when the failures of a previous generation are acknowledged. That will be a painful process for all generations.

Individual Examination: Insights about 'Sin'

Given that we are trying to look at restoration and healing, it may seem unhelpful to talk of 'sin'. Nevertheless, a failure to recognize sin can be as harmful as an over-emphasis on certain kinds of sin. We can all recognize the idea of fault, and how important it is to learn to take responsibility for what is ours. Perhaps it is less well recognized that we need to remain free of blame for what is *not* our fault. The idea of responsibility ties up with the idea of sin. We may be helped by three categories that Christian thinkers have applied to the word 'sin'.

First, there is 'original' sin. This is recognized when we simply say, 'No one's perfect'. We are far from that state which is God's will for us. However, the achievement of that perfected state is not possible for the individual alone, but is a state of total wholeness. It is only possible with the restoration of the whole created order.

Our part in that work is to remain open to love. Readiness to be hurt is a sign of love, and it is a sign of redeeming grace. In loving, we are redeemed. The world may be a mess, but we cannot escape from it. If we try, we only carry the messiness with us, or into ourselves.

The second and third categories applied to sin are 'material' sin and 'formal' sin. This distinction may seem like a lawyers' quibble, but it is a distinction that needs to be made, perhaps especially within areas of personal relationship, where boundaries are apt to be unclear, and responsibility for what happens can seem impossibly tangled. Simply put, it is the distinction between doing something which you know full well to be wrong but you do it anyway (formal sin) and, on the other hand, doing something which is morally, evidently bad, but which you may be convinced is right (material sin). In the latter case, you may in fact be free from blame, if you have taken all possible steps to inform yourself of the true facts.

Shared and Individual Responsibility

An essential step in the process of self-examination is to recognize not just what went wrong, but what one did oneself, and what was wrong in that—even when it felt perfectly OK at the time. Recognition that one did wrong may be a long time in coming, but it is a vital part of the healing process. For a Christian, this recognition should also happen in the context of a growing and deepening personal awareness of the love of God. At this point it is natural to look to see if a former partner or spouse has taken up their responsibility too. Often, however, there is no such acknowledgement. One partner seems entirely hardened to what is happening. It may be constructive to see this apparent hardness of heart as an indicator of what sort of pain they too must have suffered, at some point in their lives. Such recognition, difficult though it may be, may allow one to acknowledge their pain, and to see it as part of a process of growth unique to them, but parallel to one's own. Their process must be allowed to carry on at their own pace.

But is it necessary to talk of sin in this area at all? We may take the view that we carry our imperfection with us in all areas of life, and that our imperfection touches all parts of our humanity. However, the distinction between formal and material sin can help us to face the fact that, though we may not have intended to hurt someone in a particular situation, we nevertheless have done so and feel our responsibility. This is even more the case where we have in fact intended to cause hurt. We cannot and should not avoid responsibility. To side-step issues of responsibility, and so of sin, is to deny our continuity with our own past: ultimately, this is to deny our own humanity.

Pain, Responsibility, and a Deeper Loving

Self-examination, and owning our responsibility for mistakes, can be a saddening process if it is mishandled. The way to avoid depression, when examining our own past, and to escape either a self-loathing that is suicidal, or a self-justification that is numbing, is to accept that this mess is not the last word. From the hurt can grow a deeper loving.

A model for this is provided in the Old Testament. The people of Israel have reached the borders of the Promised Land, and are ready to enter. Spies are sent ahead, but their report discourages the Israelites, who could have conquered. Now, instead of going in God's way, they decide to invade, contrary to God's instructions, and are repulsed. This leads to a time in the wilderness, during which they have to learn dependence on God.

In telling this story, the 'promised land' should not be seen to stand for the partner in the broken relationship, but for a manner of expressing and receiving love. The time after the break-up might be viewed as a time for learning the meaning and the joy of not being independent. The prophets of the Old Testament could speak of the period in the wilderness as a time of closeness to God in simplicity.

I should never wish to seem to trivialize or patronize, but if we are to seek a 'theology of break-up' it is from this wilderness experience that we may draw. The break-up has taught us that what is desired, even what has been promised, has been denied. Yet the wilderness is not to be a resting-place. It is not the goal of the journey, but it is nevertheless a place where, with less to distract and with a spirit of humility, we may re-discover the directing love of God—and the very basic fact that we are loved, for in the wilderness there is nothing, nobody but God with us.

Transformation and a New Vision

And here is where this process is different for the Christian. Without such faith, there is the danger of self-absorption, a sense that 'it's all down to me' or 'it's all my fault'. This is where repentance is not the same as shame and self-blame. In the New Testament, the word for repentance is 'metanoia', a word that implies a changing of the mind. This will include much that has traditionally gone under the heading of 'repentance', but it will include much more beside. This change of mind will bring with it a new way of thinking about God, the world and oneself—a complete change of values and priorities.

It is the place of the Church to help those who are in the wilderness. Those who are approaching such repentance as has been described above, a re-evaluation of themselves and the world, and their values, may be helped by knowing that there is already a community in which repentance is not just first aid but a way of growth.

There is also something that the Church has to offer to its own members. Repentance of the sort mentioned is not to be an anxious picking at a scab, which will prevent healing. We are not to be deflected into an introspective anxiety. It is for us to recognize that we are made in the image of God: that is, we are made as social beings, for God is Trinity. In our failings we damage that image, but we also sometimes seek that image of ourselves and God in the wrong way, being too unsure and too inward. Our 'repentance' or transformation is to be a positive step forwards and outwards, not an anxious looking over the shoulder. Our transformation and triumph are not individualistic but shared.

The process of repentance may bring with it insight into new responsibilities. It may bring insight into previously unrecognized strengths—strengths which may also have been deliberately ignored. It should bring a recognition of weakness, but weakness without shame, for it will mean discovering how all of us are weak. From within this sense of new insight and vision, there will be a call to set aside the old idols. Has my self-image been hurtful to myself as well as others? Has my view of family life denied the humanity of someone else? Has my image of the beloved imposed impossible demands? And so on.

In this process of self-examination and self-knowing, those who have gone through the formal break-up of a partnership are no different from those who have not, and this process is ultimately more important than the ending of a marriage. We all have to grow, and growth is painful.

Conclusion

I am conscious of the enormous areas of pain that this book has tried to cover. It seems that the life journey is not a straight line, but more like a spiral, which appears to keep coming back to the same place, but in fact you are at a different level each time. Anyone who has come many years from their point of pain will know that feeling of coming back, again and again: but each time it happens, you have changed and you can face it differently.

No two individual people can be the same, and every marriage or partnership will be uniquely different. People change from moment to moment anyway, and the experience of life changes all the time. Every individual follows a path of development and growth, and sometimes that path lies within a marriage, sometimes not. No one understands the mystery of why human beings love, or fail to love, within a marriage.

In writing this book, I have tried to pass on insights about the process of growth, and the painful process of human relationship where marriage or partnership breaks down. I have incorporated my own experience and that of other adults and children. I can make no pretence to impartiality or scientific accuracy, and this account will inevitably seem biased and inadequate, to some. For this I apologize, and I am always open to thinking in a new way.

I have concentrated on the process of life, rather than on static ideas or rigid instructions. I believe that the experiencing of life is more important than any theorizing about it, and I have tried to point to the common elements of people's experiencing of divorce and separation. I have also picked out those elements of people's experiencing that consistently point towards a meaning in all the pain. In that sense of inner meaning and growth lies the only possible justification for what people suffer through the agonies of breaking up.

My belief is that the meanings we give to our experience are crucially important. Individual meanings are part of our essential humanity, and my faith is that the individual quest will inevitably lead to God, who is the meaning underlying all others.

In much the same way, I believe that the personal experience comes before the theology. In feeling our real experience, we will be freed from inadequate theories learned in school or parrot-fashion. We will come with an open spirit to truths that match our own individual and unique selves. Only in this way, I believe, do we

Conclusion

approach the state of being which is true to our deepest selves, and come to fulfil the meaning and purpose of our existence. In that fulfilling, we also fulfil God's will and make our steps within the divine dance.

In that process of discovery and growth, we encounter the profound pain of losses such as death, divorce, or impossible choices. I cannot say that all such processes of growth are good or positive. Such value-laden words seem pitifully inadequate compared with the mystery of a person's suffering, or love. But my faith is that there is a greater meaning, beyond what I can see at any one time, and especially when I am in pain. That is my faith in the future.

Further Reading

This is a brief list of some books taken from the Dawn Project resource collection. For a complete list please telephone 01709 512436.

For adults

Basciano, Christina: *Relationship Breakdown: a Survival Guide* (Ward Lock, 1977)
Biddulph, Steve: *Manhood—an action plan for changing men's lives* (Hawthorn Press, 1999)
Burgess, Adrienne: *Fatherhood Reclaimed—the making of the modern father* (Vermilion, 1997)
Cooper, J; Lewis, J: *Who can I talk to? The user's guide to therapy and counselling* (Hodder, 1995)
Fisher, Thelma: *National Family Mediation Guide to Separation and Divorce* (Vermilion, 1997)
Garlick, Helen: *The Which? Guide to Divorce* (Which? Books, 1996)
Litvinoff, Sarah: *The Relate Guide to Starting Again* (Vermilion, 1993)
Peiffer, Vera: *How to Cope with Splitting Up* (Sheldon Press, 1995)
Scarff, Maggie: *Intimate Partners* (Ballantine Books, 1987)
Wells, Rosemary: *Helping Children Cope with Divorce* (Sheldon Press, 1997)
Williams, Angela: *Divorce and Separation: Every Woman's Guide to a New Life* (Sheldon Press, 1994)

For children

Althea: *My two Families* (A&C Black, 1996)
Blume, Judy: *It's Not the End of the World* (MacMillan, 1995)
Fine, Anne: *Goggle-eyes* (Puffin, 1990)
Fine, Anne: *Step by Wicked Step* (Longman, 1997)
Grunsell, Angela: *Let's Talk About Divorce* (Gloucester Press, 1989)
Grunsell, Angela: *Let's Talk about Step families* (Gloucester Press, 1990)
Haycock, Kate: *Dealing with Family Break-up* (Wayland, 1995)
Wilson, Jacqueline: *The Suitcase Kid* (Corgi, 1996)